For Parents and Professionals™
Preschool

Marilyn A. Ianni
Karin A. Mullen

Skill Area: Language Development
Ages: 2 thru 5
Grades: PreK thru K

LinguiSystems, Inc.
3100 4th Avenue
East Moline, IL 61244-9700
1-800 PRO IDEA
1-800-776-4332

Fax: 1-800-577-4555
E-mail: service@linguisystems.com
Web: www.linguisystems..com
TDD: 1-800-933-8331
          (for the hearing impaired)

Printed in the U.S.A.

ISBN 0-7606-0275-1

Introduction

A young child learns about the world from everything he sees, hears, touches, smells, and tastes. A young child also learns about the world from every contact he has with the adults in his life. As the adults in a child's life, we have the honor of, and responsibility to, promote and nurture this growth. We indirectly foster this growth by our mere presence in the child's world through the model we provide as we interact with the world and the child. We can also choose to more directly foster this growth by assuming the role of "teacher."

As "teachers," one of the most powerful teaching tools we have to promote a child's growth is language. Language is the common thread throughout each area of a child's development. Language facilitates a child's communication skills, social development, fine and gross motor development, and cognitive growth. Language is also the common thread throughout each activity in *For Parents and Professionals: Preschool*.

The activities are also designed to promote growth in all developmental areas by involving the child in hands-on, active participation and exploration. An effort was made to target activities that are typically part of a young child's life or of high interest to a young child. Each activity promotes specific developmental skills as well as the language of each developmental area targeted. The activities are designed for children who function at an 18 – 60 month developmental level.

The activities in *For Parents and Professionals: Preschool* are divided into the following units:

> Learning Through Creative Play
> Learning Through Songs, Stories, and Gestures
> Learning Through Movement
> Learning Through Daily Routines
> Learning Through Games

Most activities have eight components. A brief description of each component follows:

The **Skills** section provides a listing of the skills (motor, language, social) addressed by the activity.

The **Materials** section lists everything you'll need to conduct the procedure. Efforts were made to include materials typically available in an early childhood setting or home or materials readily available at stores like Wal-Mart®.

The **Success Tips** are things that we have found to make the activity easier, more successful, or more meaningful.

The **Procedures** section gives directions for the primary activity (Level 1). Level 1 activities are designed for a child functioning at an 18 – 30 month level of development. Levels 2 and 3 are extensions of the Level 1 activity, and they are more complex. Level 2 activities are designed for a child functioning at a 30 – 48 month level, and Level 3 activities are designed for a child functioning at a 48 – 60 month level of development. These developmental ages are only guidelines. Decide which level is best for the child. Mix and match the levels to provide the most valuable learning experience for the child.

Each activity also has **Dialogue Highlights**. The dialogue highlights model verbal interaction for the activities. The dialogue highlights are not intended as a strict script to follow, rather they are illustrations of the differing language levels you might use as a child's language and developmental skills increase. Adapt the dialogue to meet the child's skill level.

As you proceed through an activity, attempt to keep your spoken sentences short and simple. Too much talking, or using too high a level of language may overwhelm a child. Give instructions or describe what you and the child are doing in simple terms. Repeat important parts of directions or concept words as needed. Provide pauses during which the child can initiate language and/or respond to what you are saying. Help the child gain even greater language and cognitive benefit from an activity by describing any problem solving or reasoning upon which your actions are based. Keep the rate of your speech fairly slow. Changes in inflection and loudness can demonstrate your enthusiasm and interest in an activity. Minimize the use of "No" or "Don't" during an activity. State what you want the child to do instead.

The **Extension Activity** section provides you with related, higher-level activities to further challenge the child and promote higher-level thinking skills.

The **Promoting Peer Interaction** section presents another related activity designed to promote the child's use of newly learned skills with another child or group of children. This type of interaction capitalizes on teaching in context, helps the child generalize newly-learned skills, and fosters self-confidence in peer interactions.

These components work together to provide a fun, hands-on activity which will help you in your role as the child's teacher. The components are designed to provide you with an understanding of the activity and its purpose and to provide guidance through the activity. Add your own special touch to create the most valuable learning experience for the child.

An index of the activities in each section is located on pages 179 and 180. The primary skills addressed by each activity are listed to provide a quick reference when planning activities or when attempting to target a specific skill.

Most of all, have fun!

Marilyn and Karin

Tips

When you assume the more formal role of "teacher" in a child's life, you want to be the best teacher you can be. Quality teaching is the result of a mixture of many factors. We've attempted to outline some of the factors we believe most strongly contribute to being a quality teacher.

Because each child you teach is unique and because each child's needs are unique, this list cannot be considered all-inclusive. However, it contains enough universal principles to give you a good start. You might find it helpful to read through the list periodically, in case there are some tips you want to focus on during an activity.

Teaching Tips

o   Treat the child with respect.

o   Be a nurturing person.

o   Believe in the child's capacity to change and develop.

o   Approach the child as an individual, not as a stereotype or educational "type."

o   Establish a non-threatening, enjoyable learning environment.

o   Be a perceptive observer and listener. The child has much to teach you. Observation is one of the most important ways to determine a child's strengths and needs.

o   Have a clear idea of the goal or purpose of each activity you present to the child.

o   Familiarize yourself with appropriate developmental expectations. Learn how young children develop and learn. Learn about early childhood curriculum. Match that knowledge to the content, materials, and strategies you use with the child.

o   Teaching should move from the concrete to the abstract. Learning is promoted through the use of concrete materials.

o   Don't expect a child to stay involved in an activity that is too advanced for his/her developmental ability or in an activity that is not stimulating enough.

o   Connect new information with information the child already knows. Begin the new activity by directing the child's attention to the similarities.

o   Use a variety of teaching procedures like individual skill training, demonstration, and repeated practice.

- o Use a variety of teaching materials. Change materials, toys, books, and pictures frequently.

- o Don't force a child to do an activity.

- o Remember that the finished product is less important than the process itself.

- o Provide a consistent daily schedule or routine. A child likes predictability.

- o Determine the child's best time of day. Plan more challenging activities for that time.

- o Plan ahead. Have the setting and materials for an activity ready in advance.

- o Don't waste a child's time. Don't make him/her wait.

- o Be ready to move! Learning is an active process.

- o Interact with the child on his/her level. Get down to eye level.

- o Use meaningful gestures and demonstrations. Gestures help a child understand your directions and meaning.

- o Praise the child's efforts and ideas. Don't judge, evaluate, or offer rewards ("Good try," or "I like the way you work so hard.").

- o Provide descriptive feedback ("Yes, you made <u>big</u> yellow circles. Now can you make <u>little</u> yellow circles?").

- o Give very specific feedback, both positive and negative ("Great! I said, 'clap three times,' and you went clap, clap, clap," or "Listen again. I said, 'clap three times.' You clapped two times. Can you clap three times now?").

- o Have a clear idea of acceptable behavior. Set and enforce limits. Make your behavioral expectations simple and clear, and be consistent in managing behavior.

- o Talk about, model, or gently physically guide a child through a desired behavior.

- o Promote a child's generalization of skills by looking for teaching opportunities in your daily schedule or routine (If you are working on colors, have the child help sort laundry by color.).

- o Provide opportunities for the child to do things by himself/herself.

- o Use strategies that encourage, not discourage the child.

8 　　　　　　　　　　　　　*For Parents & Professionals: Preschool*

Talking Tips

o Limit the amount of new verbal information you present at one time, particularly when working with a group of young children.

o Keep your instructions short. Demonstrate what you mean rather than talk about the task excessively.

o Work a child through an activity with a combination of coaching, prompting, and giving suggestions.

o Use variations in your voice, rate of speech, pacing, and loudness to attract and hold the child's attention.

o Listen carefully when the child communicates his/her ideas, questions, and feelings.

o Comment on the child's effort on a task ("You worked hard on your picture.").

o Report on the child's progress ("That tower is even taller than your last tower.").

o Acknowledge the child's feelings ("You're sad because your toy broke.").

o Ask questions about the child's work to show your interest.

o Ask questions to encourage higher-level thinking skills (make predictions, connect actions with events, determine causes).

o After asking a question or producing a leading comment, silently count to ten to give the child a chance to respond.

o When you present a question or a problem, encourage every response from the child.

o Ask questions to which there are no right or wrong responses ("What is your favorite _____?" or "Would you like _____?").

o Constructively enter into conversation with the child by commenting on one of the creative elements of the child's work ("You used a lot of different shapes.").

o Indicate your understanding of symbols used ("You made a lot of birds in the sky.").

o Broaden the child's self-awareness ("You made a lot of blue flowers.").

o Maintain a calm voice and demeanor when dealing with the child's behavior.

o Do not correct the child's language errors ("No, say it this way."). Respond to language errors or incomplete comments through modeling by repeating what the child has said in a more complete form. Slightly exaggerate any additions or changes you have made. Do not ask the child to imitate you unless verbal imitation is the specific goal of the activity.

o Remember there are times when remaining silent is the best thing to do!

Environmental Tips

o Provide an uncluttered work area.

o Provide a quiet work area.

o Create clearly defined work areas or learning centers.

o Have activity materials within your reach.

o Have additional materials available "just in case."

o If the child is easily distracted, place materials in a container and withdraw them as needed.

o Sit at a small table to place yourself at the child's eye level.

o Place toys and materials throughout the room at the child's level.

o Hang artwork at the child's level.

o Spread newspapers over and beneath work surfaces during "messy" activities.

Safety Tips

o Survey your work area for any safety risks. Remove any obvious risks.

o Supervise the child closely.

o Insure toys and materials used are large enough not to be a choking hazard.

o Keep dangerous supplies out of the child's reach.

o Monitor the child's use of sharp tools, such as scissors.

o Teach the child to recognize and avoid dangers.

o Teach the child to wash his/her hands regularly, particularly before cooking activities and after toileting.

o Be aware of any food or environmental allergies the child may have.

Enjoyment Tips

o Believe in the basic goodness of children.

o Choose activities that relax you. Children pick up on nonverbal cues and stress.

o Plan a "Wow" activity each day. For example, blow bubbles indoors or see how many blocks you can stack in 15 seconds.

o Share your enthusiasm with the child.

o Follow the child's lead and share his/her enthusiasm.

o Enjoyment and creativity thrive when the child is allowed to be spontaneous, messy, and silly.

o Other family members and friends may enjoy facilitating an activity.

o Make your teaching child-centered rather than based on adult interests.

o Take unconventional responses seriously.

o Dress the child appropriately for the activity. Loose, old clothes are often best.

o Spend time simply talking to the child about ideas.

o Believe in yourself.

o Be self-confident.

o Be dedicated.

o Be a decision-maker.

o Be strong, healthy, and energetic. Take care of yourself.

o Be a teacher rather than a supervisor.

Strategies for Learning Through Creative Play

> "Creativity happens all day, not just during music and art."[1]
>
> "Remember, young children learn through play . . . so never apologize when the children report, 'All we did today was play.'"[1]

What is play? Play is fun. It is a pleasurable activity for children and adults. Play is symbolic. It allows the child to go beyond the reality of the immediate world. Play is meaningful. It helps the child to relate one experience of his life to another. Play is active. It is by nature a doing, moving genre. Play is intrinsically motivated. A child's natural curiosity motivates his play. Play is voluntary. A child does not have to be forced to play. Play is rule-governed. The rules of play are sometimes those known only to the child himself while at other times, the rules are more socially dictated. Play is also flexible. It involves spontaneously shifting purposes for the child. Considering the above descriptions, it is ironic that play is often referred to as the "work" or "job" of the preschool-aged child.

Many different kinds of knowledge are being constructed through creative play. Some of these types of knowledge include:

- physical knowledge
- logico-mathematical knowledge (the understanding of relationships)
- oral and written language knowledge
- communicative competence
- social/interactive knowledge
- cognitive and curricular knowledge

Creative play is perhaps the most researched area of early childhood development. Piaget described developmental stages of play including practice play (functional play), symbolic play, games with rules, and constructions.

During the first two years of life, **practice play** dominates. Practice play is movement and the manipulation of materials for the purpose of pure pleasure. This level of play stresses the importance of pleasure over the learning of new behavior. Often children achieve a sense of confidence in their physical skills through this type of play. It is an important way the child experiments with, and learns about, his world.

Around age 2, **symbolic play** emerges and continues its development throughout adulthood. Symbolic play involves the representation of objects that are absent and pretend play. Symbolic play includes solitary dramatic play during which the child

[1]Raines, 1995.

acts out sequences of events or actions of familiar routines. Socio-dramatic play is pretend play that involves others in a joint thematic sequence (re-enacting a story). The interactions, communication, and planning that occur during symbolic play encourage the development of thinking skills.

There are many types of pretend play. During solitary pretend play, the child takes on the characteristics of an object or person or acts out a sequence. For example, the child may pretend to be an elephant. During pretend play with objects, the child uses an object to represent another object during play. For example, the child may use a cup as a telephone while pretending to call a relative. The exploration of objects precedes this type of pretend play. Other types of pretend play include pretend play with art materials, pretend play with construction materials, and pretend play with miniature buildings and people.

The type of play described as **games with rules** is typical of school-aged and older children. Games with rules usually involve a sequence that proceeds in a more formal manner until it results in a predetermined outcome. Games with rules typically define the expected action of the participants, are subject to rules, and have consequences for the violation of rules.

Constructions are described as a midway point between play and work. In this type of play, children use materials to represent reality (creating a jungle scene using paper, pipe cleaners, clay, etc. to make more realistic trees, vines, and animals).

Research indicates that active adult involvement in children's play can increase the social level of play and benefit cognitive growth. However, the adult's role is a delicate balance between promoting play without controlling the play or the child. To create and control the environment:

- make the environment stimulating, yet predictable
- have adequate space
- keep the play area well organized

When you and your workspace are organized, a child's response is more likely to be purposeful and calm.

Creating the "right" physical environment goes hand-in-hand with creating the "right" emotional atmosphere. Set consistent limits and consequences for behavior. Make the time at play predictable, creating a feeling of security and empowerment in the child.

Your choice of words is very important in helping a child understand the behavior you expect. Limit the amount you say "No" or "Don't" in play. If you have to say "No" or "Don't," follow it by a positive statement about what you want the child to do (After saying, "Don't throw the doll," you might say, "Put the doll on the chair," or after saying "Don't grab Amelia's car," you might say, "Ask Amelia if you can see the car.").

Children crave routines, repetition, and consistency. While young children may demonstrate short attention spans, they do not typically require an infinite number of choices and new surprises every day.

Make effective use of time when scheduling your play periods. Schedule activities that require concentration for the beginning of the day when the child is well rested and alert. Encourage a higher quality of play by providing long stretches of uninterrupted time. This also allows for a more creative level of play to evolve. Play periods that are too short may result in children resorting to simple, physical levels of play.

To make play even more enjoyable and successful, play at the same physical level as the child. Have materials ready and in working order. Allow the child to make some choices in the selection of materials.

Allow the child to play and become familiar with materials before encouraging a more specific manner of play. Children benefit from the freedom to explore materials in any way that interests them, within reasonable safety limits.

Provide home and daily living props such as dress-up clothes, dolls, trucks, and other vehicles to promote creative social interaction and group dramatic play. To encourage even more creativity, look at available toys and think how they may be used more interactively or in a different manner.

When facilitating play with more than one child, interact with the children to help settle problems or redirect the children to help them meet their needs. Be calm, entertaining, animated, and ready for action. Always remain flexible.

Have complete understanding of the purpose of the task in order to be ready to change the direction of the activity in response to the child's interest and the child's input during play.

Remember, you are a model for the child. The child learns many things by watching the adult he is playing with. Demonstrate or coach the child in problem solving, flexibility of thought, organizing the activity, persistence, and task completion.

There are times when more direct adult intervention in play may be necessary or even beneficial. Direct intervention may be needed when a child does not initiate or engage in make-believe play, when a child has difficulty playing with others, or when a play activity seems to be repetitious and in danger of breaking down. In these cases, you may choose to intervene using one of the following strategies:

- Parallel play: Position yourself beside the child and model appropriate play with no attempt to interact or direct play.

- Co-play: Join the existing play in progress and respond to the actions and comments of the child. The child controls the direction of play. Add to its context by asking for information.

- Play training: Take more control in direction while teaching new play behaviors.

- Thematic fantasy training: Engage the child in re-enacting favorite fairy tales and stories with predictable and repetitive plots. Thematic fantasy training benefits children who have not attempted much socio-dramatic play by modeling role-taking, pretend situations, use of imagination, and make-believe transformations. It also promotes story comprehension and competence in social skills such as turn-taking, verbal problem-solving, and negotiating.

Bubbles

Skills
- listening
- naming body parts
- coordinating eye and hand movements

Materials
- 1 cup Joy® dishwashing detergent
- 1/4 cup sugar
- plastic gallon jug
- funnel
- large, shallow bowl
- wire clothes hanger shaped into a loop for each person
- 6" square piece of panty hose for each person
- rubber band for each person

Success Tip
When doing this activity inside, prepare and play with the bubble solution over a large piece of plastic, like a tablecloth, to minimize the mess.

Procedures

Level 1

Stretch a piece of panty hose over a looped wire hanger and secure it with a rubber band. Mix the Joy® and the sugar together. Pour the mixture into the gallon jug. Fill the jug with water and pour it into the bowl.

Give the child the panty hose bubble "wand." Show the child how to dip the wand into the bubble mixture in the bowl. Then show him how to make bubbles by waving the wand.

Use words to identify body parts and locations as you talk about the bubbles. Use action words like *pop, drip, float*, and *catch* repetitively while talking about the bubbles.

Level 2

Allow the child to help you assemble the bubble soap ingredients.

Level 3

Guide the child in measuring and mixing the bubble soap.

Dialogue Highlights

Talk about what you are doing. Here are some examples.

Level 1
- *Look! Bubbles!*
- *I blow bubbles.*
- *You catch the bubbles.*
- *John popped a bubble.*

Bubbles, *continued*

Level 2
- *Let's make bubbles.*
- *Please pour the soap into the bowl.*
- *Stir the soap and sugar.*
- *Do you want to add water?*

Level 3
- *Ron, fill this cup with soap.*
- *This is a funnel.*
- *The funnel will help us put the soap and sugar into the jug without spilling it.*
- *Do you want to pour the water in?*

Extension Activity

Materials: bubble mixture, bubble wand, food coloring, white paper, spatula with holes, colander

Add food coloring to the bubble mixture. Blow the bubbles onto white paper. When the bubbles pop, talk about the shapes that remain. Then ask the child to find other objects that are shaped like a bubble. For more fun, make bubbles with other utensils, like a spatula or a colander.

Promoting Peer Interaction

Materials: bubble mixture, bubble wand, plastic bowl or cup, food coloring, white paper, crayons

Have children get into pairs. Ask one child to blow bubbles while the other child "catches" the bubbles with a plastic bowl or cup. Then have the children switch roles.

Create a joint art project. Take the children outside. Use the bubble mixture with food coloring. Ask one child to blow bubbles while the other child "catches" the bubbles on a large sheet of white paper. Have the children switch roles using the same sheet of paper. Then give the children crayons and ask them to work together to create a flower or animal using the bubble rings on the paper.

Bag It

Skills
- categorizing food
- responding to *yes/no* questions
- sorting by attributes

Materials
- grocery bag
- 6 boxes large enough to put food containers in
- foods packaged in cans, bags, boxes, and other ways
- pictures of a canned food, a boxed food, a bagged food, a refrigerator, a freezer, and a cupboard

Success Tips
Start with a small number of familiar food items.

Choose food items easy for the child to handle.

Save empty food packages to use for the activities. They also make great labels for the boxes.

If the child responds incorrectly to a *yes/no* question, model the desired response.

Procedures

Level 1 Attach a picture of a canned food to one box. Leave the second box unlabeled. Show the child several canned foods and several foods that are packaged in other ways. Talk about the foods. Next show the child the box labeled with a picture of canned food. Explain that the canned foods belong in this box. Then show the child the unlabeled box. Tell the child that the foods that are not canned belong in the unlabeled box.

Choose a canned food and ask the child to put it in the correct box. Then choose a food packaged in another way and ask the child to place it in the box where it belongs. Continue with each of the remaining food items.

Level 2 Attach pictures of a boxed food and a bagged food to separate boxes. Show the child all of the boxes, including the box with the picture of the canned food. Ask the child to place each food item in the correct box.

Level 3   Attach pictures of a refrigerator, a freezer, and a cupboard to separate boxes. Display foods that are stored in a refrigerator, a freezer, and a cupboard. Show the child the boxes. Ask the child to place each food item in the correct box.

Dialogue Highlights   Talk about what you are doing. Here are some examples.

Level 1
- *Here's some food!*
- *The peaches are in a can.*
- *I'll put the peaches in this box.*
- *Is the cereal in a can?*

Level 2
- *I'll put the peaches in the box with a can on the front.*
- *The cereal is in a box. I'll put it in the box with a box on the front.*
- *Here's a loaf of bread. Is it in a can? Is it in a box?*

Level 3
- *Some foods need to be cold, like this butter.*
- *I'll put the butter in the refrigerator.*
- *This frozen dinner needs to be very cold.*
- *I'll put the frozen dinner in the freezer.*
- *Help me put the food away.*

Extension Activities   Have the child help you put groceries away after you have gone grocery shopping. Start with a small number of items and demonstrate where the food goes. As the child becomes more skilled, she may be able to help put all the groceries away. To increase task difficulty, ask the child to name the category of food like fruit, vegetables, or dairy as she puts away the food item.

Play grocery store. Set up foods that are packaged in different ways. Give the child a grocery bag and a picture of a type of food. Have the child "shop" for the type of food in the picture.

Promoting Peer Interaction   Place all types of food on the floor. Place the boxes with pictures of a can, a bag, and a box in a different location. Provide two children with a plastic grocery bag with handles. Ask each child to hold one side of the bag. Have the children select all canned foods and place them in the bag. Then have the children carry the bag to the appropriate box and unload it. Continue this activity for the boxed and bagged foods.

Band-Aid Baby

Skills
- naming and identifying body parts
- using action words
- expanding length of utterance
- using imagination
- unwrapping and applying a Band-Aid
- comforting another "person"

Materials
- doll
- several Band-Aids in a variety of sizes
- small washtub of water
- washcloths
- soap
- towel

Success Tips
Use a clean doll to insure that the Band-Aids stick.

Use dolls with short hair, as Band-Aids may get stuck in the doll's hair.

Partially open the wrapper if the child has difficulty unwrapping the Band-Aid.

Procedures

Level 1

Demonstrate a short pretend play sequence. Explain your actions as you play with a doll that falls and gets scraped. Comfort the doll with hugs and Band-Aids. Use action words like *fall, cry, hug, pat, unwrap, help,* and *open.* Also use body part and location phrases like "on her arm," "over her eye," and "under her nose."

Then give the child the doll. Ask the child to pretend the doll fell down. Ask the child to help the doll feel better. Help the child open and put Band-Aids on the injured doll. Encourage the child to talk about the doll. Expand his comments by repeating his words and by adding more words.

Levels 2 & 3

Demonstrate the pretend play sequence described in Level 1. After the doll falls, clean the doll's "injury" with soap and water. Dry the doll and then apply the Band-Aids. Use action words to describe what you are doing. Point to the parts of the doll's body that are "hurt" and ask the child to identify the body parts.

Then give the child a doll and ask him to pretend his doll fell down. Ask him to make his doll feel better by washing the cuts and applying Band-Aids. Add words or phrases while repeating what the child says to expand his language.

Dialogue Highlights

Talk about what you are doing. Here are some examples.

Level 1

- *Look! I have a baby.*
- *Oh, no! My baby fell down.*
- *My baby hurt her arm.*
- *I hug my baby.*
- *I put a Band-Aid on her arm.*
- *Now it's your turn.*
- *Where is your baby hurt?*

Levels 2 & 3

- *My baby hurt her leg.*
- *I can help my baby feel better.*
- *I wash my baby's leg.*
- *Now I put a Band-Aid on her leg.*
- *Pretend your baby fell down.*
- *What can you do to help your baby feel better?*

Extension Activity

Materials: large sheet of butcher paper and crayons or markers

Ask the child to lie down on the paper. Trace the child's outline. Have the child apply Band-Aids to his outline. Talk about why he needs Band-Aids and where the Band-Aids are.

Promoting Peer Interaction

Develop a play sequence with one child as the doctor and the other as the caregiver. Prompt the caregiver to pretend the baby falls. Then have the caregiver bring the baby to the doctor and tell the doctor where the baby is hurt. The doctor washes the baby and puts on Band-Aids. Then have the children switch roles.

Band-Aid is a registered trademark for Johnson & Johnson, Inc.

Cereal Box Suitcase

Skills
- using a paintbrush
- following directions
- solving problems

Materials
- empty 20 oz. cereal box with flaps that close
- white spray paint
- paint shirt for each child
- paintbrushes
- 2 – 4 different colors of tempera paint
- shallow paint dish for each color of tempera paint
- decorations like stickers, doilies, glitter, ribbon, and construction paper cutouts
- tape
- several old newspapers
- stapler
- 18" of thick yarn
- marker or crayon

Success Tips
To minimize the mess when gluing decorations onto a box, pour a small amount of glue into a jar lid. Then give the child the jar lid rather than the glue bottle. Use cotton swabs to apply the glue.

If you do this activity with a large group, have the children bring their own cereal boxes.

Procedures

Levels 1, 2 & 3

Cover work surfaces with newspapers. Cover the cereal box with two light coats of white spray paint. Let dry. Pour a different color paint into each paint dish.

Show the child the cereal box covered with white paint. Explain to the child that she will make a cereal box into a suitcase by decorating the box.

Give the child the cereal box and a paintbrush. Show the child how to dip the brush into paint and how to wipe the excess paint on the edge of the paint dish. Use the occasional paint-dripping problems to help the child sharpen his problem-solving skills. Ask simple questions like, "How can we keep the paintbrushes clean?" or "What could we use to clean up spills?"

An effective way to promote verbal interaction between children is to require that the children share the materials needed to complete a project. This often provides the adult with an opportunity to model making requests and negotiating.

When the painted box is dry, encourage the child to decorate the box with ribbons, stickers, and paper cutouts. Help the child write his name on the box. Then staple yarn to each side of the box to make a handle.

Dialogue Highlights

Talk about what you are doing. Here are some examples.

Level 1

- *We're going to make a suitcase.*
- *I'll dip my brush into the paint.*
- *Now I'll put the paint on the box.*
- *You can paint the box too.*

Level 2

- *Which color do you want?*
- *You can use another color.*
- *Where does the blue brush go?*
- *Yes, it goes in the blue paint.*
- *Would it go in the red paint?*

Level 3

- *Oops, you dripped some paint!*
- *What should we do to clean up?*
- *Now the box is dry.*
- *What do you want to decorate your box with?*
- *I'll staple yarn to your box.*

Extension Activities

Materials: cereal box spray painted white, red and pink construction paper, scissors, valentines, lunch bags, gift bags

Let the child try his hand at making a valentine mailbox. Have the child decorate the box with paint, red and pink paper cutouts, and heart stickers. Let the box dry and then fill it with valentines.
For more creativity with art, have the child decorate lunch bags and gift bags. He can use cutouts, ribbons, crayons, and stickers to make the bags pretty.

Promoting Peer Interaction

Materials: a box large enough to fit two children side by side

Guide the children while they paint a box to make a car. Give each child a paintbrush. Ask the children to share one paint container. Let the paint dry. Then encourage the children to plan trips in the car, to take turns driving the car, and to pretend to repair the car.

Let's Go On Vacation

Skills
- categorizing
- self-help (packing)
- understanding the function of objects

Materials
- small suitcase
- cooler
- large box
- variety of adult and children's summer and winter clothing
- variety of food items

Levels 2 & 3
- tote bag
- variety of personal care items like toothpaste, a toothbrush, a comb, shampoo, soap, a brush

Level 3 only
- large suitcase
- one picture each of an adult, a child, a different child brushing his teeth, and a food item

Success Tips
Use photographs of the child or family members when available.

Begin the activity with a small number of items. Increase the number of items to be sorted between two categories (small suitcase and cooler) before adding a third category (tote bag).

Procedures

Level 1

Place an assortment of food items and children's clothing in the large box. Tell the child to pretend he is going on a vacation. Explain he has to pack before he can go. Show the child a small suitcase and a cooler. Open the suitcase and put a clothing item into it. Then open the cooler and put a food item into it. Talk about what you're doing.

Ask the child to choose an item from the large box. Help the child decide whether the item is clothing or food. Then encourage the child to put the item into the right container. Describe each item and its use throughout the activity.

Level 2

Ask the child what he'll need to take on his pretend vacation. Show the child the small suitcase, the cooler, and the tote bag. Choose a clothing item from the large box and put it into the suitcase. Choose a food item and put it into the cooler. Finally choose a personal care item and put it into the tote bag. Explain what you're doing as you place each item in the right container.

Ask the child to choose an item from the box. Have the child name the item. Ask the child whether he's holding something he would wear, something he would eat, or something he would use to keep himself clean. Then have the child pack the item in the correct container.

Level 3　　Tell the child he has to pack for a make-believe vacation. Show the child the small suitcase, the large suitcase, the cooler, and the tote bag. Put the pictures of the child, the adult, the child brushing his teeth, and the food item on the small suitcase, large suitcase, tote bag, and cooler, respectively.

Take turns sorting and packing items from the box. As the child chooses an item, ask him to name the item and describe its use. Then have him pack the item in the correct place.

Dialogue Highlights　　Talk about what you are doing. Here are some examples.

Level 1
- *Have you ever gone on a trip?*
- *We need to pack for our trip.*
- *We put clothes in a suitcase.*
- *We put food in a cooler.*
- *You have cookies. Do we wear cookies?*

Level 2
- *We need to pack before we go on a pretend vacation.*
- *Here are a suitcase, a cooler, and a tote bag.*
- *Look, I have a toothbrush. I'll pack things that help keep me clean in the tote bag.*
- *Help me finish packing.*
- *Pack the cookies in the right place.*

Level 3
- *How will we get ready for a vacation?*
- *We can use these suitcases, a cooler, and a tote bag to pack.*
- *I'll put the child's picture in front of the small suitcase. The small suitcase is for a child's clothes.*
- *Where will you pack the big shirt?*

Extension Activity　　Help the child learn to sort things at home or school like clothes, toys, and books. Then ask the child to put the items away.

Promoting Peer Interaction

Materials: variety of adult and children's summer and winter clothing, large box, suitcase

Put a variety of clothing items in a large box. Have the children work together to pack a suitcase. Ask one child to choose an item from the box. Encourage the children to talk about whether the item is something they would pack (a woman's sweater vs. a child's jacket). Have the other child pack the item in the suitcase. After some items have been packed, have the children switch places.

Shape Up

Skills
- identifying and naming shapes
- identifying parts of a whole
- tracing with a marker or crayon

Materials
- several paper circles, squares, and triangles
- markers or crayons
- several pictures of objects, each having only one of the above shapes like an orange, a block, or a piece of pizza

Levels 2 & 3
- several paper rectangles, triangles, and ovals
- pictures of objects, each having only one of the above shapes

Level 3
- pictures of things with more than one of the above shapes

Success Tips

Select simple pictures free of background detail.

Glue the pictures onto sturdy paper to stabilize the picture for tracing.

Work with only one shape (a circle) until the child understands the task. Then introduce a second shape (a square).

Procedures

Level 1 Outline the shape in each picture so the shapes are easier to see. Show the child a paper circle. Trace the shape with your finger. Talk about the shape. Let the child take turns tracing the circle with his finger. Next show the child the square and the triangle. Trace each shape with your finger and talk about the shape. Let the child trace the shapes with his finger. Then show the child a picture of an object with a circle shape in it. Name the object and its shape. Talk about the shape and trace it with a marker or crayon. Let the child trace the shape too. Repeat the activity with the square and the triangle.

Level 2 Show the child the paper shapes. As you and the child trace the shapes with your fingers, talk about them. Then have the child trace the shapes with a marker and name them. Show the child a picture of an object with the circle shape in it. Ask the child what the object is and what shape he sees. Outline the shape with your finger or a marker. Next give the child another picture of an object with a circle shape in it and a marker or a crayon. Encourage the child to find the circle shape in his picture. Then ask him to trace the shape. Repeat the activity for the square and the triangle.

Creative Play
For Parents & Professionals: Preschool

Level 3   Show the child the paper shapes. Talk about each one. Ask the child to name each shape as you hold it up. Then show the child a picture that has more than one shape in it like a house. Name each shape and trace it with a marker. Then give the child another picture with more than one shape in it. Have him trace each shape with a marker. Ask him to name the picture and the shapes.

Dialogue Highlights   Talk about what you are doing. Here are some examples.

Level 1
- *This is a circle.*
- *I'm tracing the circle with my finger.*
- *You made a circle too.*
- *Here's a picture of an orange. It's shaped like a circle.*
- *Watch me trace around the orange with my crayon.*
- *You trace around the orange.*

Level 2
- *The circle goes round and round.*
- *What shape did you trace?*
- *What shape do you see in the clock?*
- *Watch me trace the circle in the clock.*
- *Now I want you to find the circle in your picture.*
- *Find the square in this picture.*

Level 3
- *We talked about circles, squares, triangles, rectangles, and ovals.*
- *There are many shapes in this house.*
- *Look at the windows. They look like squares.*
- *Can you find another shape on the house?*

Extension Activities   Materials: child-sized scissors, simple pictures

Have the child cut out the shapes in simple pictures along traced lines. As the child masters the activity, provide pictures with more detail, and have the child find and trace all the shapes in the picture.

Look at labels on food in the cupboard or refrigerator. Find and name the shapes on the labels. Trace the shapes with a marker.

Promoting Peer Interaction   Materials: paper or plastic bag, paper shape cutouts

Put paper shape cutouts in a bag. Have one child pick a paper shape from the bag and give it to the second child. The second child hunts for an object with that shape. When the children agree on a match, have them switch roles.

Shapely Pictures

Skills

- recognizing and naming shapes
- combining parts to make a whole
- tracing
- cutting
- gluing

Materials

- large sheet of construction paper
- simple shapes cut out of construction paper
- glue

Levels 2 & 3

- simple shapes traced onto pieces of construction paper
- scissors
- crayons or markers

Level 3

- shape patterns of a circle, a square, a triangle, a rectangle, an oval, and a diamond
- scraps of colored construction paper, wrapping paper, or wallpaper

Success Tips

Use a wide-tipped marker to trace the shapes to be cut.

Use a quarter or half-sheet of construction paper per shape. Give the child one shape at a time to cut out.

When tracing shape patterns, use a loop of masking tape to hold the pattern in place.

Procedures

Level 1   Show the child the circles, squares, and triangles. Talk about things that are made of different shapes such as how an ice-cream cone looks like a circle and a triangle. Show the child how to make an ice-cream cone shape picture by gluing a circle and a triangle onto a sheet of construction paper. Ask the child to name the shapes.

Then give the child the materials to make his own shape picture. Encourage the child to tell what his picture is and what shapes he used to make his picture. Use a marker to outline the shapes as he names them.

Asking the child to turn a picture upside-down to create a different picture encourages flexibility in perception and thought.

Level 2	Give the child scissors, crayons, and papers with circles and squares traced on. Help the child cut out the shapes. Give the child additional cutout shapes. Show him how to use shapes to make pictures as described in Level 1 (ice-cream cone). Ask the child to add details like grass or flowers to his picture. Trace the shapes in the picture with a marker. Then talk about the child's picture and the shapes used to make it.
Level 3	Show the child how to trace the shape patterns. Have the child trace and cut out shapes. Have the child watch as you make a picture using shapes. Name the shapes you use to make each part of your picture. Then rearrange the shapes to make a new picture. Ask the child to choose the picture he liked most. Glue the shapes onto your paper to make the chosen picture. Use crayons to trace the shapes and add details to the picture. Then encourage the child to use his shapes to make a picture.

Dialogue Highlights   Talk about what you are doing. Here are some examples.

Level 1
- *Look at the circles, squares, and triangles.*
- *Watch me make a picture with some shapes.*
- *I'll glue a circle onto my paper. It looks like ice cream.*
- *Next I'll glue a triangle onto my paper. It looks like a cone.*
- *I'll outline the shapes in my ice-cream cone.*
- *You can make your own shape picture.*
- *Let's outline the shapes in your picture.*

Level 2
- *I made an ice-cream cone with a circle and a triangle. Now it's your turn to make pictures.*
- *Cut out your circle and square.*
- *Use them with these other shapes to make a picture.*
- *Tell me the shapes in your picture.*

Level 3
- *Let's make shapes today with these shape patterns.*
- *I'll hold this pattern on my paper. Then I'll use my crayon to draw around the outside of the shape.*
- *I'll use my scissors to cut out the circle.*
- *Now you make your own shapes.*
- *I can make a picture with my shapes.*
- *I'll mix up the shapes and make a different picture.*
- *I'll glue the shapes onto my paper.*
- *Watch me trace the shapes.*
- *Now you can use your shapes to make your own shape picture.*

**Extension
Activity**

Materials: paper shapes, glue, additional art supplies (pipe cleaners, glitter, and buttons)

Name a category like animals or vehicles. Ask the child to make an item in the category using paper shapes. Then provide more art supplies like pipe cleaners, glitter, and buttons. Have the child turn his picture upside down and create a new picture from the original picture using the additional art supplies.

**Promoting
Peer
Interaction**

Have each child select two shapes. Ask the children to combine their shapes to create an object. Allow the children to decorate their object with crayons and markers.

You Look Marvelous

Skills
- dressing
- sharing
- playing cooperatively
- following directions

Materials
- full-length mirror
- assortment of adult and child-sized clothing and accessories

Success Tip
Use clothing and accessories that are easy to put on like hats, mittens, shoes, purses, and jewelry.

Procedures

Level 1   Put the clothing and accessories in an open area in front of the mirror. Tell the child the name of each item as you try it on. Ask the child to try on the clothing and accessories. Be ready to help the child if needed. Give the child simple directions like "Put on the necklace," or "Put on this mitten."

This activity is more interactive and fun when the adult also dresses up.

Level 2   Show the child some of the clothing and accessories. Ask the child to name each item and to talk about where you wear it. Encourage the child to try on the clothing and accessories in front of the mirror. Give the child directions like "Put the red sock on your foot," or "Put the flowered hat on your head." When the child consistently follows your directions, try giving silly directions like "Put the mitten on your foot," or "Put the hat on your knee." Encourage the dressed-up child to look in the mirror and talk about how he looks.

Level 3   Add more details or give longer directions. You might say, "Put the red hat on my head, put the flowered hat on your head, and put the ring on your finger." When the child consistently follows your directions, try giving silly directions like, "Take the mitten off your hand and put it on your foot," or "Put two hats on my knees." Ask the child to look at himself in a mirror and to talk about how he looks.

Dialogue Highlights   Talk about what you are doing. Here are some examples.

Level 1
- *Look! I have a hat. I put it on my head.*
- *It's time to put on clothes.*
- *Look in the mirror.*
- *You have a hat on your head.*

Level 2
- *Look! What is this? Yes, it's a hat.*
- *Now you can dress up.*
- *Put the purse on top of your head. That's silly! What do you wear on your head?*

Level 3
- *Do you want to dress up?*
- *Put the red shoe and the blue shoe on your feet.*
- *Now take the bracelet off your wrist and put it on your nose.*
- *Let's look in the mirror. What do you see?*

Extension Activities

Materials: large box, clothing items and accessories, timer, doll, doll clothes

Have a dress-up relay race. Place a box with four clothing items and accessories at one end of the room. Set a timer for 3 – 5 minutes. Tell the child to race to the box, put on all of the clothing and accessories, pick up the box, return to start, and remove the clothing and accessories before the timer rings.

Give the child a doll and several clothing items. Ask the child to dress her doll according to your directions. You might give simple directions like "Put the shoes on the doll," or more difficult directions like "Trade your doll's shirt with my doll's shirt."

Promoting Peer Interaction

Ask one child to put on three clothing items and accessories out of sight of the second child. Have the first child put one item on in a silly place. Then have the second child tell the first child which items he put on and which item is in a silly place. Have the second child tell where the item should be worn. Have the children switch roles.

Be My Baby

Skills

- using imagination
- exploring adult roles
- playing cooperatively
- practicing personal care routines
- following directions
- imitating or creating a pretend play sequence

Materials

- two baby dolls (one for the child and one for you)
- box big enough to hold a doll
- bottle and blanket for each doll

Level 2
- assortment of baby care items (clothing, spoon, bowl, bib, Velcro®-tab diaper)

Level 3
- assortment of baby care items based on the roles selected (thermometer, stethoscope, bottle)

Success Tips

Use larger baby dolls to make it easier for the child to handle the doll.

Encourage a child's play to become more complex by adding new steps to an existing play sequence.

Procedures

Level 1 Give the child a doll and hold one yourself. Encourage the child to pretend his doll is a real baby. Tell the child it's the babies' bedtime. Use a sequence similar to the following to get your baby ready for bed. First wrap your baby in a blanket. Then give your baby a bottle. Finally give your baby a goodnight kiss, and put her to bed in the box. Encourage the child to copy what you do. Talk the child through each step.

Level 2 Have the child role-play putting the child to bed. Then ask the child to feed his baby using a spoon, play games like *So Big* or *Pat-A-Cake*, or diaper his baby. Offer props and suggestions for each new activity. When the child has practiced different pretend play options with his baby, experiment with more roles.

Level 3 Explore adult roles outside the home. Ask the child to pretend he is the baby's doctor or grandparent and you are the baby's parent. Give the child guidelines for each role. Encourage longer and more complex play sequences for each role. The doctor may take the baby's temperature, weigh the baby, give the baby a shot, or talk to the parent.

Dialogue Highlights

Talk about what you are doing. Here are some examples.

Level 1

- *Here is a baby doll.*
- *I have a doll too.*
- *Get your baby ready for bed.*
- *I'll wrap my baby in a blanket.*

Level 2

- *Pretend your doll is a real baby.*
- *Your baby is awake. I think she's hungry.*
- *Here is a bowl, spoon, and bib.*
- *Wipe your baby's face after she eats.*

Level 3

- *I'll be the baby's dad (mom) and you be the doctor.*
- *What will you do to check my baby?*
- *Good, you weighed the baby and gave him a shot.*
- *Now can you look in the baby's ear to see if he has an earache?*

Extension Activity

Give the child stuffed animals instead of dolls. Have the child pretend he is part of the animal's family. Ask the child to take care of the baby animal. Use materials readily available to represent objects commonly used with a baby or animal. For example, you might use a pencil to represent a needle to give the baby a shot.

Promoting Peer Interaction

Have two children share one baby. Ask one child to be the parent and the other child to be a sibling or a grandparent. Give the children guidelines for their pretend play. For example, tell the children the baby is tired. Ask the "parent" to direct the second child in completing a care routine. Then have the children switch roles.

Let's Do Lunch

Skills
- using imagination
- exploring adult roles
- playing cooperatively
- practicing personal care routines
- following directions
- imitating or creating a pretend play sequence

Materials
- bowls and spoons

Level 2
- glasses, plates, napkins, pans

Level 3
- materials based on the role the child selects for play

Success Tips

Before beginning this activity, read books about families or talk about the child's family routines. For example, you might read *The Best Time of Day* by Valerie Flournoy.

Sitting on the floor or in a child-sized chair will encourage greater interaction between you and the child.

Procedures

Level 1   Ask the child to pretend it's time for breakfast. Put a bowl and a spoon in front of you. Tell the child to do the same. Pretend to pick up a cereal box and pour cereal into your bowl. Then pretend to pour milk on the cereal. Pick up the spoon and pretend to eat the cereal.

Designate an area as a pretend sink. Put your dirty dish and spoon into the sink. Encourage the child to copy what you do. Talk the child through the steps. Repeat this pretend play sequence with the child fixing cereal for both of you and then washing the dishes.

Level 2   Ask the child to pretend it's time for lunch. Give the child pans and spoons. Designate areas as a pretend stove and a pretend sink. Ask him to cook lunch. Then give the child glasses, plates, and napkins. Ask him to set the table. Talk about what you like to eat. When the child is finished cooking, ask him to bring the make-believe meal to the table. Encourage him to pretend to pass the food around, fill your plates, and eat. Follow the meal with clean-up. You may need to model the pretend play sequences or offer suggestions like, "Why don't you cook the spaghetti? You can make the sauce," and "You can make a cake for dessert."

Level 3	Complete the activity as described in Level 2. Then explore other household activities like going to the grocery store. Let the child decide what he'll do. If he can't decide, offer suggestions. Encourage the child to act out his new role.

Dialogue Highlights

Talk about what you are doing. Here are some examples.

Level 1

- *It's time for breakfast.*
- *Let's eat cereal. We need bowls and spoons.*
- *I'll pour the cereal into my bowl.*
- *Good, you're pouring milk too.*

Level 2

- *It's time for lunch.*
- *Here are some pans and spoons.*
- *Let's pretend this chair is a stove.*
- *What are you going to make?*
- *Set the table while the macaroni cooks.*
- *What a delicious lunch!*
- *Why don't you wash the dishes and I will dry them?*

Level 3

- *Lunch is over. There is no food left.*
- *What do we need to do?*
- *What will we buy at the grocery store?*
- *Good, you're making a list.*

Extension Activity

Ask the child to pretend it's someone's birthday. Pretend to have a party, complete with birthday dinner, cake, and presents. Allow the child to put on dress-up clothes. Or have a formal dinner party or picnic.

Promoting Peer Interaction

Materials: a pad of paper, a pencil, a large sheet of paper folded in half as a menu, uniform props like a bill cap or an apron

Ask the children to play restaurant. Have one child be the customer and one child be the waiter. Talk about each role. Guide the play as needed. Suggest sequences like presenting the menu, writing down the food order, and asking what the customer wants to drink. Then have the children switch roles.

Yield for Fun

Skills
- using imagination
- imitating or creating a pretend play sequence

Materials
- toy cars
- blocks

Level 3
- large sheet of sturdy paper
- toy figures
- variety of vehicles
- markers

Success Tips

Help the child drive a toy car by placing your hand over his until he understands the play sequence.

Cover completed play mats with lamination or clear contact paper to preserve them.

Procedures

Level 1   Use blocks to create a road and buildings. Name the buildings as you create them. Take a car and drive to different locations along the road. Have the child's car follow your car. Talk about where you're going and what you're doing at each location. Encourage the child to copy what you do.

Level 2   Give the child the blocks. Have the child make a road and buildings. Ask the child to begin driving. Follow him with your car. Ask questions and talk about what the child is doing as he stops at each building.

Level 3   Introduce toy figures and additional vehicles like emergency vehicles and dump trucks. Assist the child in drawing roads on a large sheet of sturdy paper to create a play mat. Use blocks to make a building for each vehicle. Name each building. Ask the child to begin driving the vehicles. Ask questions and talk about the action the child creates at each building.

> *In pretend play, a child often likes to repeat a play sequence many times. Use your judgment to determine when it is time to expand or change that play sequence.*

Dialogue Highlights	Talk about what you are doing. Here are some examples.

Level 1
- *I'm going to make a road.*
- *Put the blocks together.*
- *I'm making a house.*
- *Now I'm making a restaurant.*

Level 2
- *Here are some blocks and cars.*
- *Can you make a road on the floor?*
- *What other buildings can you make?*
- *Let's drive.*
- *You stopped at the library. What did you do there?*

Level 3
- *Look! I have people and more cars and trucks.*
- *What is this car?*
- *Let's draw roads on this paper for the cars and trucks.*
- *Now make some buildings.*
- *Which vehicle will you drive first?*
- *Where are you going?*

Extension Activity

Materials: additional sheet(s) of sturdy paper, tape, scissors, glue, magazines

Tape a second sheet of sturdy paper to the first sheet of paper to expand the play mat. Reinforce the seams by placing tape on the top and bottom of the seam. Draw connecting roads, bridges, and parks. Add new buildings on the expanded mat. Glue pictures cut from magazines to create scenery. Continue to play with the child as described in Level 3.

Promoting Peer Interaction

Using the play mat and a variety of vehicles, assign each child a specific role that requires him to work with another child. For example, tell one child his car is broken or out of gas and another child he is a mechanic, or have children be a fast-food worker/customer or police officer/robber. Listen to the dialogue between the children and help them expand their roles as needed.

40

Creative Play
For Parents & Professionals: Preschool

Talking Hands

Skills
- developing pre-handwriting skills
- expressing the words *down, up, side,* and *round*
- understanding direction concepts
- recognizing features

Materials
- can of shaving cream
- tray or cookie sheet

Success Tips
Use an old adult-sized shirt buttoned down the back as an apron to protect the child's clothing.

If a washable surface is not available for this activity, use an oil cloth or vinyl tablecloth.

Procedures

Level 1   Place a mound of shaving cream on a tray or cookie sheet. Help the child put his hands into the shaving cream. Talk about how the shaving cream looks and feels. Help the child move his hands up and down on the work surface. Use the words *up* and *down* to talk about what the child is doing.

Level 2   Encourage the child to put his hands into the shaving cream. Ask the child to move his hands around the work surface. First show the child how to make vertical strokes. Show the child how to move his hand up and down using his whole arm. Then show him how to refine his movements until he is making vertical strokes with one finger. Repeat the activity for horizontal and then circular strokes.

Children improve hand-eye coordination by making vertical, horizontal, and circular strokes in the shaving cream.

Level 3   Encourage the child to put his hands into the shaving cream. Have the child talk about how the shaving cream looks and feels. Ask the child to move his hands up and down, side to side, and round and round. Then have him refine his movements until he's making strokes with one finger. As the child masters the arm and finger movements, show him how to make checks, crosses, squares, and letters. Encourage him to make different designs in the shaving cream. Then have the child talk about his designs.

Talking Hands, *continued*

Dialogue Highlights

Talk about what you are doing. Here are some examples.

Level 1

- *Look! I have shaving cream!*
- *I put your hands in the shaving cream.*
- *The shaving cream feels cold.*
- *Move your hands up. Move your hands down.*
- *Up and down. (Side to side. Round and round.)*

Level 2

- *We're painting with shaving cream!*
- *The cream is cold.*
- *We're moving the shaving cream up and down (side to side, round and round).*
- *You made a beautiful picture.*

Level 3

- *You can move your hands up and down. You can move them side to side or round and round.*
- *Tell me how the shaving cream feels.*
- *Now move your fingers like this.*
- *Tell me about your picture.*

Extension Activities

Materials: colored bath foam, window cleaner*, a cleaning cloth

Have the child use colored bath foam to make designs in the bathtub or on the wall of a shower. Encourage him to move the foam up and down, side to side, and round and round. Try some other designs too.

Ask the child to help you dry mirrors and windows. At first, guide the child's hands to move up and down, side to side, and round and round. Then let the child dry the mirrors and windows on his own.

*An alternative to using commercial window cleaner is this non-toxic mixture: Two teaspoons white vinegar to 1 quart water in a spray bottle.

Promoting Peer Interaction

Materials: balloon, tape, shaving cream, plastic spoon

Inflate a round balloon, tie it, and tape the end to a washable work surface. Ask one child to stabilize the balloon with both hands while the second child spreads shaving cream over the balloon. Have the children take turns holding the balloon and drawing designs like faces on the balloon. Then have the children take turns "shaving" the face with a plastic spoon.

Creative Play
For Parents & Professionals: Preschool

Snakes, Spiders, and Snails!

Skills
- improving small muscle control
- using action words

Materials
- play dough
- plastic containers for storage

Level 3
- play dough tools like a rolling pin, cookie cutters, and plastic knives

Success Tip
Homemade play dough may become sticky. Have a small bag of flour available to add to the dough to make it firmer.

Procedures

Level 1
Show the child how to pound, press, and poke the play dough. Have the child touch the play dough. Encourage him to poke his fingers into it, press it flat, or pound it using both hands. Talk about what the child is doing with the play dough.

Level 2
Challenge the child to make fun play dough shapes. Show him how to shape the play dough into simple forms like a ball, a pancake, or a pizza. Then give the child his own play dough. Encourage him to roll the play dough with open palms to create a snake. Encourage the child to talk about what he's making with his play dough.

Level 3
Challenge the child to make more complex shapes. Give the child some play dough and have him make a snake. Try coiling the snake's tail and shaping the snake's head to make it stay upright. You might also form spiders by pressing rolled strips of play dough onto the edges of a pancake-shaped piece of play dough. Encourage the child to use play dough tools to be more creative. Have him talk about what he's doing and making.

Dialogue Highlights
Talk about what you are doing. Here are some examples.

Level 1
- *Here is play dough.*
- *I can pat the play dough. Pat, pat, pat.*
- *Now I'm going to poke the play dough.*
- *It feels soft.*
- *Here is your play dough.*
- *We can pound the play dough. Pound, pound, pound.*

Level 2

- *I can roll the play dough. I made a ball.*
- *Now I'll pound the play dough. What did I make?*
- *Here's play dough for you. What can you make?*
- *What else can you make with your play dough?*

Level 3

- *Roll the dough to make a snake.*
- *Your snake is skinny, like mine.*
- *I can make his head stay up.*
- *Look at the tools.*
- *Let's use them to make something else.*

Extension Activities

Make your own play dough with the child by combining the following in a saucepan:

1 c. flour
1/2 c. salt
2 t. cream of tartar
1 c. water mixed with a few drops of food coloring
1 T. cooking oil

Cook over medium heat, stirring constantly until the mixture forms a ball. Knead until smooth. Let the play dough cool thoroughly before giving it to the child. Store the play dough in an airtight container. This recipe is non-toxic and the play dough keeps for weeks.

For more dough fun, have the child shape cookie dough into animals. Use chocolate chips, raisins, and sprinkles to make features. Bake according to recipe directions. Eat and enjoy!

Promoting Peer Interaction

Materials: a bowl, a non-stick baking sheet, an oven, refrigerated dough like pizza, biscuit, or breadstick dough

Separate the dough into pieces and place in the bowl. Place the baking sheet between the children. Ask the children to use the dough to create one masterpiece. Bake according to package directions. When cool, let the children decide whether to eat or to save their creation.

Strategies for Learning Through Songs, Stories, and Gestures

> "Children enjoy repeating words and sentences, not for understanding and communicating, but for the sake of playing with the rhymes and songs or words and sentences."[1]
>
> "Get back to the basics. Sing, dance, tell a story."[2]

Songs and fingerplays provide a fun way to enhance children's communication skills. For variety in singing experiences, children should have the chance to sing with recordings, with instruments, and on their own without accompaniment.

When teaching songs to children, choose songs about things that are familiar to the child and that have lyrics consistent with the child's language ability. Begin with short, simple songs. Sing the song for the child two or three times, then invite the child to join in. Children enjoy songs with repeated phrases. When teaching a longer song, you might ask the child to echo each line or phrase back to you. Repeating the song will help it become part of the child's repertoire.

Body language is the first type of language used and understood by humans. Teaching fingerplays allows the child to actively participate while learning the language.

When selecting fingerplays to teach, begin with simple actions that are repeated, like clapping in *If You're Happy and You Know It*. Next use whole body movements, like touching body parts in *Head, Shoulders, Knees, and Toes*. Then introduce smaller movements with hands and fingers, like *The Eensy Weensy Spider*. Sitting behind the child may make it easier for you to assist with hand movements.

Keep the activity interesting by making faces, varying the pitch and tone of your voice, and varying the volume of your voice.

Favorite songs and fingerplays can be used to entertain the child during idle minutes, like waiting in line at the store, driving in the car, or during transitions from one activity to the next at school.

Words and motions for fingerplays are found following the lesson that mentions songs and fingerplays. Additional fingerplays can be found on pages 72 – 75.

Reading books together is one of the most pleasurable ways for you to spend time with a child. When selecting books to read to preschoolers, it is essential to select books appropriate for the child's communication abilities.

[1]Maffei and Hauck, 1992.
[2]Raines, 1995.

Strategies for Learning Through Songs, Stories, and Gestures, *continued*

Start with books having one object pictured per page. Realistic illustrations or photographs are best. These books are more "naming" books than stories and are an excellent choice for first books. They can also be used later on to encourage vocabulary development. Look at the books with the child as you name each picture. After the child is familiar with the object pictured, enhance the activity by describing the object. "This is a ball. The ball is red. You like to throw balls." Or point out details in the picture, "This is a car. Here are the wheels. This is the door."

Wordless picture books can also be used to encourage a child's imagination and vocabulary development. These books can help children understand that the sequence of a story is important, as they must focus on the details of the picture to know the story.

When selecting books, look for books that are small enough for the child to handle easily. Cardboard pages make it easier for small hands to turn the pages. Features like flaps or pop-ups offer surprises and encourage the child to participate.

First storybooks are characterized by good illustrations that predominate the page and a few lines of text. Look for repetition and repeated phrases within the text and predictability for what comes next. These books may focus on categories such as vehicles, colors, or animals, and present many examples of items from the category.

Next look for stories with simple plots (often a problem and the solution to the problem) or books that describe a familiar life sequence like going to Grandma's. These stories have a central character and often teach a moral lesson. While there may be several lines of text per page, illustrations are still important.

When introducing a new book to a child, you may want to spend some time looking at the cover first. Read the title to the child. Talk about the cover illustration. Ask the child what he thinks might happen in the story. It is helpful if you have read the book and are familiar with the sequence of the story.

Other considerations when reading with children:

- To develop attentiveness, try reading several short books instead of one long one.

- Consider the audience. Are you reading to one child or to a group of children? When reading to a group, select a larger book with big illustrations. If you are able to tell the story or can read upside-down, hold the book in front of you to make it easier for the children in a group to see. You may want to use props or flannel cutouts to tell a story to a group rather than relying on a book that may be hard for all to see.

                                        For Parents & Professionals: Preschool

- Establish a routine for reading. A regular time for reading makes reading as much a part of the child's day as lunch and bedtime. Choose a quiet place away from distractions for reading activities. Store books in a bin that is accessible to the child.

- Keep your voice interesting. Use different voices for each character.

- Select books about topics of particular interest to the child.

- If the child loses interest, it's okay to finish the book another time.

To make reading experiences extra-special:

- Use the child's name for the main character in the story.
- Share a favorite story from your childhood.
- Ask the child to "read" a favorite story to you.
- Help the child make up a new ending for a favorite story.

Developmental Sequence for Songs, Stories, and Gestures
○   turns pages of book, 2 – 3 at a time
○   names one picture
○   turns pages singly
○   points out specific objects in pictures
○   joins in nursery rhymes
○   names self in photograph
○   uses gestures to demonstrate use of common objects
○   listens to 5 – 10 minute story
○   imitates a sequence of three actions or movements
○   recalls the order of a familiar story by pointing to the picture of "What comes next?"
○   names three items in a complex picture
○   uses gestures to show actions like eating, running, and sleeping
○   repeats four lines of a simple nursery rhyme

Sing That Song

Skills
- repeating simple words or phrases
- completing familiar phrases
- remembering a musical rhythm
- following game rules

Materials
- tape or CD of familiar children's songs
- tape or CD player

Success Tips

Highly repetitive, simple children's songs like *London Bridge, Are You Sleeping?, Where is Thumbkin?,* and *If You're Happy and You Know It* are perfect for this activity.

Humming the melody is one way to prompt the child to remember the next word or phrase of the song.

Procedures

Level 1   Play a song and ask the child to listen. Stop the song before a simple, repetitive word. Have the child sing the next word of the song with you. Continue the song and the activity. Introduce another familiar song and repeat the activity. When the child is consistently singing the repetitive word with you, introduce movement. Have the child start walking in a circle when the music starts. When the music stops, have the child stop walking. Then have her sing the repetitive word.

> *"Nursery rhymes, songs, and poems that children have heard and enjoyed many times are important materials for introducing children to reading."*
> (Kostelnik et al., 1993)

Level 2   Follow the procedure described in Level 1 to teach the child an entire repetitive phrase in a song. When the child is able to sing the repetitive phrase with you, take turns singing the repetitive phrase when the music stops.

Level 3   Follow the procedure described in Level 1 to teach the child longer and less repetitive lines of a song. When the child is able to sing the line with you, take turns singing the line when the music stops.

Dialogue Highlights

Talk about what you are doing. Here are some examples.

Level 1

- *Listen to the song.*
- *Let's sing it together.*
- *I'll play* Twinkle, Twinkle, Little Star *again.*
- *I stopped the tape.*
- *What comes next? The word* star *comes next.*
- *Now I'll play it again.*
- *This time, walk in a circle when the music starts.*
- *When the music stops, you stop.*
- *The music stopped.*
- *Now let's sing.* Twinkle, twinkle, little . . . *What comes next?*

Level 2

- *I'll play the song about* Bingo. *You listen.*
- *When I stop the tape, we'll sing the next line.*
- There was a farmer had a dog. *What comes next?*
- And Bingo was his name-o.
- *Let's listen some more.*
- *Your turn.*

Level 3

- *What song do you want to sing?*
- *Okay, we'll sing* Hickory, Dickory, Dock.
- Hickory, Dickory, Dock. *What comes next?*
- The mouse ran up the clock. *Let's sing it.*
- The mouse ran up the clock. The clock struck one.
- *Sing what comes next.*

Extension Activity

Materials: tape recorder

Ask the child to make up new words or phrases to finish familiar songs. Tape-record your new version of a favorite song. Include pauses to allow the child time to sing the next word or phrase.

Promoting Peer Interaction

Sing a familiar song with two children like *Row, Row, Row Your Boat.* Explain to the children that you'll each sing a different line of the song. Start singing the song. Point to each child when it's her turn to sing. It might be fun to sing the last line together.

49

Songs and Fingerplays

London Bridge

London Bridge is falling down,
Falling down, falling down.
London Bridge is falling down,
My fair lady.

Are You Sleeping?

Are you sleeping? Are you sleeping?
Brother John. Brother John.
Morning bells are ringing. Morning bells are ringing.
Ding, ding, dong. Ding, ding, dong.

Where Is Thumbkin?

Where is Thumbkin?	*(Hands behind back.)*
Where is Thumbkin?	
Here I am.	*(Bring right hand from behind back with thumb sticking up.)*
Here I am.	*(Bring left hand from behind back with thumb sticking up.)*
How are you today, sir?	*(Have thumb on right hand bend up and down as if "talking" to other thumb.)*
Very well, I thank you.	*(Have thumb on left hand "talk" to thumb on right hand.)*
Run away.	*(Put right hand behind back.)*
Run away.	*(Put left hand behind back.)*

Continue with other fingers (pointer, tall man, ring man, pinky).

If You're Happy and You Know It

If you're happy and you know it, clap your hands.
If you're happy and you know it, clap your hands.
If you're happy and you know it, then your face will surely show it.
If you're happy and you know it, clap your hands.

Continue with stomp your feet and shout "Hurray."

50

Songs, Stories, and Gestures
For Parents & Professionals: Preschool

Twinkle, Twinkle Little Star

Twinkle, twinkle little star,
How I wonder what you are.
Up above the world so high,
Like a diamond in the sky.
Twinkle, twinkle little star,
How I wonder what you are.

Bingo

There was a farmer had a dog
And Bingo was his name-o.
B-I-N-G-O,
B-I-N-G-O,
B-I-N-G-O
And Bingo was his name-o.

There was a farmer had a dog
And Bingo was his name-o.
(Clap)-I-N-G-O,
(Clap)-I-N-G-O,
(Clap)-I-N-G-O
And Bingo was his name-o.

Repeat the song, clapping instead of saying the first two letters of Bingo's name
(Clap-clap)-N-G-O). Continue repeating the song, clapping for the first three letters
of Bingo's name, then four letters of Bingo's name, then clapping for all the letters of
Bingo's name.

Hickory, Dickory, Dock

Hickory, dickory, dock.
The mouse ran up the clock.
The clock struck one.
The mouse ran down.
Hickory, dickory, dock.

Row, Row, Row Your Boat

Row, row, row your boat
Gently down the stream.
Merrily, merrily, merrily, merrily,
Life is but a dream.

51

The Rest of the Story

Skills

- creating a story ending
- listening to a story
- sequencing events in a story
- answering simple questions
- telling a story ending
- predicting story events

Materials

- Story Starters, page 54

Success Tip

Introduce props from the story to help the child remember the story line.

Procedures

Read the first story starter to the child.

Level 1   Help the child finish the story by offering choices. You might ask the child whether there is a ball or a book in the box. Continue asking questions and offering choices until the child has built an ending for the story. Then retell the story starter and add the child's ending. Next time, use the same story starter or choose a new story starter.

Level 2   Ask simple questions to help the child finish the story. You might ask the child which present she would like to find in a box. Continue asking questions and gathering ideas until the child has built an ending for the story. When the story is complete, retell the story starter and add the child's ending. Next time, use the same story starter or choose a new story starter.

Level 3   Ask the child what will happen next. Encourage the child to build on the story starter to create a story. Ask questions if necessary. When the child has finished her story, have her retell the story starter and the ending she created. The retold version is sometimes wilder than the original! Next time, use the same story starter or choose a new story starter.

Songs, Stories, and Gestures
For Parents & Professionals: Preschool

Dialogue Highlights

Talk about what you are doing. Here are some examples.

Level 1

- *I take off the lid, look inside, and see . . .*
- *What's in the box?*
- *Is it a ball or a book?*
- *It's a book.*
- *A storybook or a coloring book?*
- *It's a coloring book.*
- *I get out my crayons.*
- *Do I color a cow or a house?*

Level 2

- *I take off the lid, look inside, and see . . .*
- *What's in the box?*
- *You see a car in the box.*
- *What happens next?*

Level 3

- *I take off the lid, look inside, and see . . . What?*
- *Then what happened?*
- *What happened after that?*
- *I like that story.*
- *Tell me the whole story again!*

Extension Activity

Materials: child's favorite book

Ask the child to choose a favorite book. Read the story. Then read the first part of the story as a story starter. Ask the child to make up a new ending to the story.

Promoting Peer Interaction

Select a story starter. Using the procedure from Level 1, have the children develop a story that includes a character for each child. Assign each child a role in the story. Have the children act out their story.

Story Starters

1. Today's my birthday! I'm opening the biggest present first! I pull off the bow and tear off the paper. I take off the lid, look inside, and see . . .

2. John was in bed. He was almost asleep when he saw something move on his floor! He looked again. It was his backpack! His backpack was jumping across the floor! John got up, opened his backpack, and saw . . .

3. I love it when Mom picks up her car keys and says, "Let's go!" That means we're going for a ride in the car. Funny things happen when we ride in the car! The last time we went for a ride, we . . .

4. David and Jenna played baseball in the park. Jenna swung the bat and hit the ball. The ball went so far that it landed in the woods. David ran into the woods to find the ball. He looked and looked. Jenna went to help him. David and Jenna didn't see the ball, but they did see . . .

5. Charles and Rachel liked to play outside. They liked to dig in the dirt with shovels. One day, they decided to see who could dig the biggest hole. Suddenly, Charles yelled, "Come here, Rachel! Look what I found!" Rachel ran over to the hole Charles had dug. She saw . . .

Silly Syllable Stories

Skills
- imitating words or phrases
- making early developing consonant sounds
- promoting auditory memory skills
- clapping in time to a chant

Materials
- Silly Syllable Stories, page 57

Success Tip

A child often enjoys hearing herself on tape. Help the child record herself saying the silly syllable stories. Encourage her to use the tape to practice the stories by herself.

Procedures

Repeat a Silly Syllable Story a few times to the child. Show the child how to keep time with the story by clapping her hands, snapping her fingers, or tapping her feet.

Level 1   Encourage the child to say any words in the story. Next time, use the same Syllable Story or choose a new Syllable Story.

Level 2   As the child becomes familiar with the Silly Syllable Stories, pause before the final word in each line. Have the child repeat the last word. Continue to practice each story until the child can say the last line of each story without help.

Level 3   When the child becomes familiar with the Silly Syllable Stories, encourage the child to say the stories by herself. Supply missing words as she recites each story. For more fun, ask the child to make up a different word to end each story.

Dialogue Highlights   Talk about what you are doing. Here are some examples.

Level 1
- *Listen! I'll tell you a silly story.*
- *Did you like the silly story?*
- *Listen again. You can help.*
- *Clap your hands. (Snap your fingers. Tap your feet.)*
- *Listen again!*
- *Help me say the words.*

Level 2
- *Listen to the silly story again.*
- *This time I'll stop and you say the last word.*
- Ball. Big . . . *Great! You said, "ball."*
- *Can you say the last line before I do?*

Level 3
- Pretty, pink pigs pop . . .
- *Can you think of a different word to end this story?*
- *You said, "Pretty, pink pigs pop Popsicles®!"*
- *Can you think of a different word now?*

Extension Activity

Write your own Silly Syllable Stories. Start the words of the story with sounds like *b, w, p, m, n, d,* or *t*.

Promoting Peer Interaction

Have the child teach a friend one of the Silly Syllable Stories.

Silly Syllable Stories

Ball
Big ball
Baby's big ball
Baby's big ball bounces.
Baby's big ball bounces bye-bye.

We
We want
We want wet
We want wet warm
We want wet, warm worms.

Pigs
Pink pigs
Pretty, pink pigs
Pretty, pink pigs pop
Pretty, pink pigs pop popcorn.

My
My mess
My muddy mess
My muddy mess makes
My muddy mess makes Mom
My muddy mess makes Mom mad.

Two
Two tiny
Two tiny turtles
Two tiny turtles tiptoe.
Two tiny turtles tiptoe to town.

57

Fingerplay Fun

Skills
- imitating actions
- imitating words
- remembering a sequence of phrases or actions
- expanding length of utterance

Materials
- simple fingerplays with few lines and lots of repetition of words and actions like *Open, Shut Them* and *Head, Shoulders, Knees, and Toes* (See page 60.)
- additional fingerplays (optional), pages 72 – 75

Success Tips

You may need to practice at a slower pace until the child is familiar with the fingerplay.

Begin with fingerplays that allow the child to remain seated.

Continue to practice previously learned fingerplays while you introduce new fingerplays.

Procedures

Seat the child facing you. Model the actions and words as you say each line of the fingerplay. Repeat the fingerplay and invite the child to imitate your actions.

Level 1　　You may need to put your hands on the child's hands to help her perform the actions. Repeat the fingerplay for several days until the child does the actions by herself. Then introduce another fingerplay.

"As children move into the preschool years, they begin to understand moving to music . . . as a form of nonverbal communication."
(Jalongo, 1996)

Level 2　　When the child can spontaneously do the actions, encourage her to say the repetitive words or lines or the last word of the line. Pause to give the child a chance to say the repetitive words or last word of the line. Repeat the fingerplay for several days until the child does the actions and repetitive lines by herself. Then introduce another fingerplay.

Level 3　　When the child can spontaneously do the actions, encourage her to say all the lines. Repeat the fingerplay for several days until the child does the actions and lines by herself. Then introduce another fingerplay.

Dialogue Highlights

Talk about what you are doing. Here are some examples.

Level 1

- *Watch my hands.*
- *Listen.*
- Open, shut them. Open, shut them. Give a little clap.
- *Now move your hands with me.*
- *Ready?* Open, shut them. Open, shut them. Give a little clap.
- *Good! You clapped by yourself.*

Level 2

- *Good for you! You did all the actions that time.*
- *Now listen to the words.*
- *Can you say some of the words with me?*
- Open, shut them. Open . . . *Yes!* Shut them.
- Give a little . . . clap. *That's right!*

Level 3

- *You really like* Open, Shut Them.
- *You can do all the actions by yourself.*
- *I bet you can do all the words by yourself too.*
- *I'll help you get started. Ready?* Open, shut them.

Extension Activity

Create fingerplay actions to a familiar song. Ask the child to choose a favorite song. Say each line of the song and pick an action or actions for that line. Repeat the song and actions until the child is able to perform by himself.

Promoting Peer Interaction

Teach the children a fingerplay like *Eensy, Weensy Spider* or *Five Little Monkeys*. Then have the children face each other. Tell each child to put her fingertips against the other child's fingertips. As you repeat the lines of the fingerplay, help the children modify the actions of the fingerplay to allow them to keep their fingertips together. Repeat the fingerplay and actions until the children can perform the fingerplay without adult assistance.

Words / Actions to Fingerplays

Open, Shut Them

Open, shut them.	*(Open and shut fingers.)*
Open, shut them.	*(Open and shut fingers.)*
Give a little clap.	*(Clap hands once.)*
Open, shut them.	*(Open and shut fingers.)*
Open, shut them.	*(Open and shut fingers.)*
Put them in your lap.	*(Place hands in lap.)*
Creep them, crawl them.	*(Walk fingers up the child's chest.)*
Creep them, crawl them,	
Right up to your chin.	*(Put fingers on child's chin.)*
Open wide your little mouth,	*(Have child open his / her mouth.)*
But do not let them in!	*(Hide hands behind your back.)*

Variation:

Roll them, roll them.	*(Roll hands.)*
Roll them, roll them.	*(Continue to roll hands.)*
Roll them, just like this.	
Wave them, wave them.	*(Wave hands.)*
Wave them, wave them.	*(Continue to wave hands.)*
And blow a little kiss.	*(Blow a kiss.)*

Head, Shoulders, Knees, and Toes
(Sung to the tune of "London Bridge")

Touch each body part as it is said.

Head and shoulders, knees, and toes;
knees and toes; knees and toes.
Head and shoulders, knees, and toes;
eyes, ears, mouth, and nose.

Five Little Monkeys

Five little monkeys jumping on the bed.	*(Two fingers from right hand "jumping" on left palm.)*
One fell off and bumped his head.	*(Hold up one index finger. Place other hand on head.)*
Mama called the doctor and the doctor said,	*(Put thumb by ear and pinky by chin as if talking on a phone.)*
"No more monkeys jumping on the bed!"	*(Shake one index finger.)*

Repeat with four, three, two, and one monkey(s).

Feelings

Skills
- identifying emotions
- recognizing how another person feels
- sharing feelings with others
- talking about emotions
- understanding the feelings *happy, sad, angry,* and *scared*

Materials
- pictures of a happy person, a sad person, an angry person, and a scared person
- mirror

Level 2
- bulletin board
- thumbtacks
- Polaroid® camera and film

Success Tip
Portray extremes of each emotion as you begin this activity.

Procedures

Level 1 Show the child a picture of a happy person. Talk about the person's smile and other things that make the person look happy. Smile and ask the child to copy your happy face. Have the child look at her face in a mirror. Say the word *happy*. Continue talking about how people look and feel using the pictures of the sad person, the angry person, and the scared person.

Level 2 Show the child the picture of the happy person. Ask the child whether the person is happy, sad, angry, or scared. Talk about the person's smile and the things that make the person look happy. Then ask the child to look happy. Encourage her to look at her happy face in the mirror. Talk about how she looks. Continue talking about how people look and feel using the pictures of the sad person, the angry person, and the scared person.

Hang the pictures on the bulletin board. Then take photos of the child. Tell the child to look happy, sad, angry, and scared. Give the child one of her photographs and have her describe how she looks in the photograph. Have the child pin her photograph near the picture on the bulletin board showing the same emotion. For example, if the child looks at her photo and says, "Happy," have her pin her photograph near the picture of the happy person.

When the child has hung all her photographs, point to the picture of the happy person. Have the child make a happy face. Ask her whether she looks happy, sad, angry, or scared. Repeat this activity with the pictures of sad, angry, and scared people.

Level 3   Tell the child you're going to learn about what a person does with her whole body when she feels angry, happy, sad, or scared. Assume a pose with your arms folded across your chest, your weight evenly balanced on your legs. Stare directly at the child with a furrowed brow. Have the child tell you what you are doing with your arms, your legs and feet, and your head and face. Talk about each part of your pose. Ask the child to identify the feeling you are showing. Then have the child imitate your pose. Continue with the feelings happy, sad, and scared.

Dialogue Highlights   Talk about what you are doing. Here are some examples.

Level 1
- *Look! He's happy.*
- *Look at his smile. Look at his eyes.*
- *I'm happy too.*
- *Can you make a happy face?*
- *Yes, your face looks happy.*
- *Look at the picture again.*
- *Does the man look happy? Yes! He's smiling.*
- *Let's both look happy now. Smile.*

Level 2
- *Look at this person.*
- *Is this person happy, sad, angry, or scared?*
- *This man is happy. He's smiling and his eyes are open wide.*
- *Can you look happy too?*
- *Look in the mirror. You're smiling. You look happy.*
- *Here's another picture.*
- *Who's in this picture? It's a picture of you!*
- *Look at your picture.*
- *Do you look happy, sad, angry, or scared?*
- *You look happy.*
- *Hang your picture near the picture of the happy person.*

Level 3
- *I can tell from a person's face whether he is happy, sad, angry, or scared.*
- *Let's look at what our bodies do when we're angry.*
- *How am I holding my arms? Right. They're crossed.*
- *Now look at my legs and feet.*
- *How do they look? They're very straight.*
- *What am I doing with my face?*
- *You're right. I'm staring at you.*
- *My forehead is all scrunched up. It has lines in it.*
- *How do you think I feel? Yes! I'm angry.*
- *Now you do what I do.*

Extension Activity

To help the child learn to identify her own feelings, use words to describe them whenever the child shows an emotion. You might say, "You're crying. You look sad. What's wrong?" You can also point out emotions when looking through books or watching TV/videotapes.

Promoting Peer Interaction

Have the first child stand in front of a friend. Quietly tell the first child to make her face and body appear happy, sad, angry, or scared. Ask the second child to decide if the first child looks happy, sad, scared, or angry. Have the second child tell how she knew what the first child was feeling. Prompt the second child to talk about the first child's arms, legs and feet, and head and face. Then have the children switch roles.

Act It Out

Skills

- remembering the sequence of a story
- using imagination
- repeating lines from a story
- playing cooperatively
- performing for an audience

Materials

- familiar children's storybook with a simple plot, a few characters, and lots of repetition, like *The Little Red Hen, The Three Bears, The Three Pigs*, or *The Three Billy Goats Gruff*
- any props necessary for the story you choose

Success Tip

Use different voices for each character while you read or narrate the story.

Procedures

Read the story to the child for several days before the activity.

Level 1   Read the story and stop after repetitive words. Encourage the child to repeat the words of one or two characters in the story with you.

Level 2   When the child is familiar with the story, teach her actions to act out the story. When the child consistently does the actions to the story, she's ready to perform.

Read the story as the child acts. Modify the story to include the child's name. You might read, "Abby was the little goat. She went across the bridge." Do the story actions as you read and encourage the child to copy what you do. Pause after repetitive words and encourage the child to repeat the words. When you've finished the story, show the child how the audience would clap. Show her how to take a bow.

Level 3   Read the story and encourage the child to say repetitive words or phrases without your help. Pause before turning each page to ask the child, "What will happen next?" As the child becomes familiar with the story, teach her the actions to act out the story. Read the story like a script. You might say, "And then the wolf said . . ." Let the child supply the words and actions for the wolf. When the child consistently supplies these words and actions, she's ready to perform. Talk about what she'll say and do.

Introduce the characters and let the child fill in the dialogue and actions. Help the child if she forgets what to say or do as you narrate. You might say, "Abby saw a little house. What did she say? What did she do?"

Dialogue Highlights	Talk about what you are doing. Here are some examples.

Level 1

- The little billy goat went across the bridge.
- Trip-trap. Trip-trap.
- *You said, "Trip-trap." Good job.*
- *Now let's trip-trap. Watch me.*
- Trip-trap! Trip-trap! Abby came to the bridge.
- Abby was the littlest goat.
- Abby went trip-trap, trip-trap!
- *You said, "Trip-trap."*
- *Now walk across the bridge.*
- *Good job! Let's clap!*

Level 2

- And then the wolf . . . *Can you say the next part?*
- *Yes, the wolf huffed and puffed!*
- *Let's huff and puff! Good job!*
- *Now you'll be the wolf.*
- *What does the wolf do when she sees a house?*
- The wolf went to the house.
- The pigs didn't let the wolf in, so she . . .
- *That was a fun play!*
- *Let's clap.*

Level 3

- Papa Bear looked at his bowl. What did he say?
- *Good!* He said, "Who's been eating my porridge?"
- *What will happen next?*
- *What will the bears say?*
- *What will the bears do?*
- *Yes, the baby bear will cry.*
- Papa Bear said . . .
- Then Mama Bear said . . .
- And Baby Bear said . . .
- *Good job! You said the words for all the bears!*
- *Let's act out the play.*
- *You be the Papa Bear. What will you say when you see your chair?*

Extension Activity	After the child has performed several times with you, have her perform for others.
Promoting Peer Interaction	Using the procedures described above, assign different roles to each child. Practice until all children are ready to perform.

By the Book

Skills

- sequencing pictures
- listening to a story
- retelling a story

Materials

- worn, short storybook with many pictures and little text (a sewn binding works best)
- three-hole paper punch
- three-ring binder
- scissors

Success Tip

Check to see if the pages of the book are numbered before you take it apart. If it isn't, lightly number the pages of the story on both sides with a pencil.

Procedures

Read the story aloud and point out details in each picture. Then talk about the worn condition of the book. Explain that you'll take apart the pages and put them back together. Be sure to tell the child that this is a special activity. Explain she shouldn't take apart other books. If the book's binding is sewn, snip the threads. Invite the child to help pull threads out of the binding. Then take the pages out of the book. Show the child how to use the paper punch to put holes in the pages. Encourage the child to help you punch the holes.

"The single most important activity for building the knowledge required for eventual success in reading is reading aloud to children."
(Anderson et al., 1985)

Level 1   When the storybook pages are taken apart and hole-punched, retell the story. Hold up the first page and tell the first part of the story. Then hold up two pages as you tell the next part of the story. Ask the child to choose the picture that illustrates the part of the story you told. If the child can't choose the picture, help her point out one or two details in the picture that illustrate the part of the story you told. When the child chooses the correct picture, put it into the binder. Continue telling the story and adding pages to the binder. When all the pictures are in the correct order in the binder, retell the story and show the pictures to the child.

Level 2   When all the pages are taken apart and hole-punched, keep the first page and spread out the other pages in front of the child. Show the first page to the child and retell the part of the story that's illustrated by the picture. Then ask the child to find the picture that shows the next part of the story. When the child recognizes the next picture, ask her to put the page into the binder as you tell the corresponding part of the story. If the child doesn't realize she's holding the next page, tell the next part of the story and talk about what the picture looks like. Continue adding pages to the binder as you tell the story. When all the pictures are in the binder, read the story again. For an extra challenge, ask the child, "What happens next?" before turning each page.

Level 3

When all the pages are taken apart and hole-punched, keep the first page and spread out the other pages in front of the child. Ask the child to help you tell the story again. Explain that you'll begin the story because you have the first page. Tell the child to find the next page of the story. Have her tell that part of the story. Alternate telling the story with the child. After telling your part of the story, ask the child, "What happens next?" Wait for the child to tell the next page of the story. If the child doesn't recognize she has the next page, give a clue about the next part of the story and the corresponding picture. After the child has told her part of the story, have her add her page to the binder. When the book is complete, read it. Pause after each page to ask, "What will happen next?"

Dialogue Highlights

Talk about what you are doing. Here are some examples.

Level 1

- *Look! Here's a book.*
- *Listen while I read the book.*
- *This book is old.*
- *Let's take it apart.*
- *Watch. I'm cutting the strings.*
- *Pull the strings.*
- *The pages are apart. Let's put them back together.*
- *Look at this page.*
- The three bears went for a walk.
- Then Goldilocks knocked on their door.
- *Look at these two pictures.*
- *Is Goldilocks knocking in this picture?*
- *No, she isn't. This page isn't next.*
- *Is Goldilocks knocking in this picture? Yes, she is!*
- *This is the next page. I'll put it in the binder.*

Level 2

- *This book is old.*
- *Let's take it apart. Then we can put the pages back together.*
- *Here's the first page of the story.*
- The porridge is too hot, so the three bears took a walk.
- *Do you have the page that comes next?*
- After the bears went for a walk, Goldilocks knocked on their door.
- *Do you have the picture that shows Goldilocks knocking on the door?*

Level 3
- *We took apart the book. Now we need to put it back together.*
- *I'll keep the first page.*
- *Here is a page for you.*
- *Now we'll tell the story and we'll put the pages back together.*
- *I have the first page, so I'll start telling the story.*
- *You'll help me finish the story.*
- The porridge was too hot, so the three bears took a walk.
- *What happens next?*
- *Do you have the next picture?*
- *Tell me what happened after the bears went for a walk.*

Extension Activity

Materials: construction paper, markers or crayons, tape

After reassembling the book, ask the child to draw a cover for the story. Tape the cover to the binder. Display your "new" book for others to see.

Promoting Peer Interaction

Conduct the activity as described in Level 3. Divide the pages among all of the children.

Hand Jive

Skills
- patterning
- sequencing
- memory

Materials
- sheet of paper (optional)
- pencil (optional)

Success Tip

Don't ask or expect the child to say the letters as she learns the sequences of movements.

It is helpful to write down the patterns you are going to teach (A-A-B, A-A-B [clap, clap, tap thighs] or A-B-A-B [snap fingers, touch nose]).

Procedures

Level 1   Tell the child you are going to teach her a game to play with her hands. Ask the child to copy the way you move your hands. Clap your hands together once. If the child does not spontaneously clap, gently guide her hands through the movement. Call this gesture (one clap) "A." Refer to this movement as "A" each time you use it. When the child is consistently able to imitate one clap, tell the child to watch how many times you clap. Slowly clap two times while saying "A-A." Ask the child to imitate you. If the child does not spontaneously clap twice, gently guide her hands through the two movements. Talk about the number of times you clapped and the number of times she will clap. Continue to practice at this level until the child is able to consistently imitate when you clap twice. Then mix your presentation of one or two claps at a time until the child is able to consistently imitate you. Repeat this process to teach the child to imitate three claps. Then teach her to imitate a mixture of sequences of one, two, or three claps in a row.

Level 2   Introduce a second hand movement like tapping your hands on your thighs palm down. Call this hand movement "B" and refer to this movement as "B" each time you use it. When the child is consistently able to imitate tapping her hands on her thighs, tell the child you will make a pattern of two hand gestures for her to imitate. Demonstrate a slow sequence of one clap and one tap on your thighs. Say the letters of the sequence ("A-B") while you make the hand gestures. Have the child imitate you.

Have the child watch and then imitate the number of times you produce the A-B sequence. Practice with a mixture of one, two, or three sequences in a row (A-B-A-B, A-B-A-B-A-B, etc.) until the child is consistently able to imitate your gestures the correct number of times.

Then introduce a third hand movement like tapping fingertips. Call this hand gesture "C." Refer to this hand movement as "C" each time you use it. Teach the child an A-B-C pattern and continue the activity as described in the paragraph above. As the child masters this level, speed up your presentation of the sequence.

Level 3   Challenge the child to imitate different combinations of A, B, and C hand movements like A-A, B-B, A-B, A-C, B-C, A-A-B, A-B-A, B-B-C, etc. When the child is consistently able to imitate different sequences, practice with a mixture of two or three of these sequences in a row as described in Level 2.

Dialogue Highlights   Talk about what you are doing. Here are some examples.

Level 1
- *Let's play a hand game.*
- *Watch me.*
- *I clap my hands one time. A.*
- *You clap your hands.*
- *Now I clap two times. A-A.*
- *You clap two times. A-A!*

Level 2
- *I'll clap my hands one time and tap my legs one time.*
- *You copy me. Do it just like I do.*
- *Watch.*
- *A-B-A-B. (Clap and tap as you say the letters of the sequence.)*
- *Your turn.*
- *A-B.*
- *I did it two times, A-B-A-B. You do it two times, A-B-A-B.*

Level 3
- *Get ready to watch.*
- *B-B-C, B-B-C! (Tap and touch nose as you say the letters of the sequence.)*
- *Your turn.*
- *B-B-C, B-B . . . don't forget C.*
- *Let's do it again.*
- *B-B-C, B-B-C.*
- *Your turn.*

Extension Activity

Create other examples of simple patterns like A-B, A-A, B-B, or A-B-C. For example, line up a row of red and green blocks, alternating colors. Point to each block and describe the pattern as A-B-A-B-A, etc. Then describe the pattern by saying, "red-green-red-green, etc." You might also create a pattern of cans (A) and jars (B) with groceries.

Promoting Peer Interaction

Direct a group of children to line up to create different patterns. Begin a simple pattern like boy-girl-boy (A-B-A) and ask the next child to get in line to continue the pattern. Assist the children as needed to create the correct part of the pattern. You might also ask the children to line up with hands up-hands down or facing front-facing back, etc. When the line is complete, point to each child and describe the pattern.

Additional Fingerplays

When I Was . . .

When I was one year old,	*(Hold up one finger.)*
I was very small.	*(Crouch on the floor.)*
Now I'm three years old (four, five).	*(Hold up three [four, five] fingers.)*
I'm very, very tall.	*(Stand up and stretch with hands high above head.)*

Five Little Ducks

Five little ducks went swimming one day,	*(Hold up five fingers.)*
Over the hills and far away.	*(Put hand behind your back.)*
Mother duck said, "Quack, quack, quack."	*(Tap fingertips together to show the mother duck "quacking.")*
Four little ducks came swimming back.	*(Bring hand from behind back showing four fingers.)*

Repeat with four, three, two, and one duck(s). When one little duck doesn't come swimming back, end with "No little ducks came swimming back." Then continue with:

Sad Mother duck went swimming one day,	*(Make a sad face.)*
Over the hills and far away.	*(Put hand above eyes like looking for something far away.)*
Mother duck said, "Quack, quack, quack."	*(Tap fingertips together to show "quacking.")*
Five little ducks came swimming back.	*(Bring hand from behind back showing five fingers.)*

Two Little Feet

Two little feet go tap, tap, tap.	*(Tap feet.)*
Two little hands go clap, clap, clap.	*(Clap hands.)*
A quick little jump from the chair,	*("Jump" up from chair.)*
Two little hands fly up in the air.	*(Put hands in the air.)*
Two little fists go bump, bump, bump.	*(Thump fists on knees.)*
Two little feet go jump, jump, jump.	*(Jump up and down.)*
One little body turns round, round, round,	*(Turn around.)*
And little child sits quietly down.	*(Sit down.)*

Grandma

These are Grandma's glasses,   *(Circle eyes with thumbs and forefingers.)*
And this is Grandma's cap.   *(Join hands above head and rest on head like a cap.)*

This is the way she folds her hands,   *(Fold hands.)*
And puts them in her lap.   *(Place hands in your lap.)*

Eensy, Weensy Spider

The eensy, weensy spider
Went up the water spout.   *(Have the spider "climb."*)*
Down came the rain and
Washed the spider out.   *(Wiggle fingers as you move your hands down in front of your face.)*

Out came the sun and
Dried up all the rain,   *(Form hands into a circle over your head.)*
And the eensy, weensy spider
Climbed up the spout again.   *(Have the spider "climb" again.)*

*To make the spider "climb," put fingertips on left hand to thumb on right hand. Turn hands so fingertips on right hand touch thumb on left hand. Continue turning hands so fingertips and thumbs touch as the spider "climbs."

This Is the Way
(Sung to the tune of "This Is the Way We Wash Our Clothes")

Act out each motion as it is mentioned. Have fun making up your own!

This is the way we comb our hair, comb our hair, comb our hair.
This is the way we comb our hair, so it will look nice.
This is the way we brush our teeth . . . so we can smile bright.
This is the way we wash our faces . . . so we will be clean.
This is the way we dress for school . . . we need to wear our clothes.
This is the way we eat our breakfast . . . to grow strong and healthy.
This is the way I cover my mouth . . . when I have to cough.

Ten Little Fingers

This is a good "quieting" fingerplay to prepare for reading or another quiet activity.

I have ten little fingers, they all belong to me.	*(Show all fingers.)*
I can make them do things, do you want to see?	*(Hands on hips, bend forward.)*
I can open them up wide, shut them tight.	*(Spread fingers wide, then pull them back together.)*
Put them together, put them out of sight.	*(Clap, then hide your hands.)*
Jump them up high, jump them down low.	*(Put hands in the air, then put hands down by the floor.)*
Put them together and place them just so.	*(Fold hands together, then put them in your lap.)*

The Wheels on the Bus

The wheels on the bus go round and round,	*(Move hands in a rolling motion.)*
Round and round, round and round.	
The wheels on the bus go round and round,	
All through the town.	*(Spread hands / arms out as if to show an area.)*

Continue with these verses:

The people on the bus go up and down, . . .	*(Stand up and then sit down.)*
The babies on the bus go wah, wah, wah, . . .	*(Pretend to cry.)*
The mommies (or daddies) on the bus go shh, shh, shh, . . .	*(Hold finger to lips.)*
The wipers on the bus go swish, swish, swish, . . .	*(Move arms back and forth.)*
The doors on the bus go open and shut, . . .	*(Hands up, palms facing away. Move hands apart [open] and together [shut].)*
The lights on the bus go blink, blink, blink, . . .	*(Flick fingers.)*

A Little Turtle

There was a little turtle.	*(Clasp hands together.)*
He lived in a box.	*(Hold clasped hands away from body.)*
He swam in a puddle.	*(Dog paddle with hands/arms.)*
He climbed on the rocks.	*(Place one palm down flat. "Walk" fingers across knuckles.)*
He snapped at a mosquito.	*(Press heels of palms together. Open*
He snapped at a flea.	*fingers and snap shut for each line*
He snapped at a minnow	*or have child clap.)*
And he snapped at me.	
He caught the mosquito.	*(Pretend to catch something with hands.)*
He caught the flea.	*(Pretend to catch something with hands.)*
He caught the minnow,	*(Pretend to catch something with hands.)*
But he didn't catch me!	*(Put hands behind back and shake head "No.")*

Strategies for Learning Through Movement

"Movement is the first language of children. Through it, they express themselves and their curiosity for the world around them."[1]

Being in motion seems to be a natural state for many young children. Even as babies, movement is important in expressing wants and needs, communicating moods, and for finding out about the world. During the preschool years, children learn and refine a wide array of motor skills. First children learn to move, then they move to learn.

The activities in this section provide a variety of movement experiences. Some focus on practical skills, helping to develop basic movement skills. Others are games that require using motor skills in a group setting. The rest involve creative movement and teach the child to express feelings and ideas through physical gestures.

A child's motor skills develop from head to toe, from the trunk to the extremities. Therefore, children begin throwing and catching before running or kicking. It is important for adults to know the order in which motor skills are acquired. Emphasis should not be placed on learning skills by certain ages, rather adequate time and opportunity must be given for motor skills to develop in the appropriate sequence. Adults must observe children closely, watching for clues that a skill has been mastered and that it is time to move on.

Adults play key roles in the success of movement activities.

- Plan appropriate activities ahead of time. Children should be actively participating most of the time. Avoid games where children must wait for their turns.

- Organize all equipment before beginning an activity. Have adequate materials for the number of children participating.

- Define the space to stay in during the activity.

- Provide a safe play area with mats or carpeted areas as needed. In the classroom, move tables, chairs, or other equipment to provide a clear play area.

- Use clear directions to explain the activity.

- Establish limits for the use of materials.

[1]Seefeldt, 1992.

For Parents & Professionals: Preschool

- Use verbal cues to prompt the child.

- Teach the motor skills required first, then conduct the activity.

- Begin with simple activities that grow more complex as skills improve.

- Modify the activity as needed to accommodate the children.

The equipment is as important as the activity.

- When teaching catching skills, start with a large foam ball, slightly deflated playground ball, or beanbag.

- When teaching throwing skills, start with a small foam ball or tennis ball.

- With any activity using a ball, you can make the activity easier or harder by varying the speed that the ball is thrown, rolled, or kicked.

- Vary the settings for practice to insure mastery of the skill. For example, play catch inside with beanbags or balloons, or outside with playground balls or foam balls.

Be a participant in the activity.

- Demonstrate the skills needed for the activity for the child.

- Help the child perform the skill. Hold the child's hand or arm for jumping or hopping. Stand behind the child and place your hands over hers to help with throwing or catching.

- Play along when introducing the activity, then withdraw as the child is comfortable participating with the group.

Developmental Sequence for Movement

o   rolls ball while in sitting position

o   throws small ball

o   goes up and down 4 – 6 steps holding onto railing or with hand held, placing two feet on a step

o   walks up to and kicks a large ball

o   stands on one foot for one or two seconds

o   jumps in place one or more times

o   walks up three or more steps, alternating feet

o   catches a large ball

o   kicks a large ball rolled toward her

o   hops on one foot at least two times

o   catches a bounced ball

o   bounces a large ball to someone four feet away

o   kicks stationary ball to target

o   throws ball overhand at least 15 feet

Ready, Set, Actions

Skills
- imitating actions
- using action words
- building vocabulary

Materials
- pictures that show familiar actions like walking, hopping, and driving

Level 2
- brown grocery bag

Level 3
- the comics page from the newspaper

Success Tip
For Level 3, enlarge the comics on a copy machine to make it easier for the child to see.

Procedures

Level 1   Show the child an action picture. Name the action and show the child how to do it. Ask the child to do the action with you. Encourage the child to look at the picture and do the action on his own.

Play a variation of the game *Charades*. Look at two action pictures. Tell the child you'll do one of the actions and he'll choose the picture showing the action you did. Encourage him to name the action. Then show the child two different action pictures. Have the child take a turn performing the action for you to identify.

Level 2   Put the action pictures into a bag. Tell the child to take a picture from the bag. Ask him to look at it without showing it to you. Then tell the child to perform the action pictured. Guess which action the child performed. Alternate taking turns until all pictures have been used.

Level 3   Point to different actions pictured on the comics page from the newspaper. Then act out one of the actions. Ask the child to find the comic frame showing the action you did. Have him name the action and then name the character doing the action. Accept non-specific names like "a mom" or "the dog." Ask the child to think of another person or thing that might perform the same action. For example, if the child identified you acting out a bird flying, you might say, "What else flies?"

Then have the child take a turn acting out an action pictured on the comics page. Let him direct you to name the action and to find the character doing the action. Then prompt the child to ask you the question about another person or thing that might perform the same action. Answer the question.

Dialogue Highlights

Talk about what you are doing. Here are some examples.

Level 1

- *Look at this picture.*
- *A boy is hopping.*
- *Watch me hop.*
- *Now you hop.*
- *Good! You're hopping too.*
- *Look at my pictures.*
- *This is a girl running. This picture is a bird flying.*
- *Watch. I'll do one of the actions.*
- *Which one did I do?*
- *Yes, I was flying.*
- *You take a turn.*

Level 2

- *I'll put the pictures in the bag. You choose one.*
- *Look at it, but don't show it to me.*
- *Put the picture down and turn it over so I can't see it.*
- *Now do the action. I'll guess what you are doing.*
- *I think you were driving. Was I right?*
- *Show me the picture.*
- *Yes, I was right. You pretended to drive.*

Level 3

- *Here's the comics page.*
- *Oh look, this bird is flying. Here is a mom cooking.*
- *I'll pick one to act out. Then you guess which one I acted out. Ready?*
- *You're right. I was flying.*
- *Who was flying in the comics?*
- *Yes, the bird was flying.*
- *What else flies? Right, an airplane flies.*
- *Now you find a comic to act out.*
- *I think you're running.*
- *Tell me to find the comic with running.*
- *The dog is running.*
- *Now ask me "What else runs?" Children run too.*

Extension Activity

Materials: TV, VCR, child's favorite video

Tell the child that you and he are going to act out parts of his favorite video. Show a portion of the video to the child. Turn off the video and talk about the scene. Have the child name the actions performed in the scene. Then act out the scene with the child.

80

Movement
For Parents & Professionals: Preschool

Promoting Peer Interaction

Materials: action pictures, bag

Play a *Follow the Leader* game. Put several action pictures in a bag. Have one child take a picture from the bag. Then have him start the game by saying, "Ready, set, (name of the pictured action)." For example, if the child chooses a picture of a boy hopping, he'll say, "Ready, set, hop!" Then all the children should hop. Give each child a turn to be the leader.

Shadow Dancing

Skills
- using the words *fast* and *slow*
- moving your body through space
- spatial relationships

Materials
- tape player or CD player
- tape or CD with music that varies in tempo
- spotlight, flashlight, or projector
- large area with a blank wall

Level 3
- large sheets of white paper
- tape
- wide-tipped marker

Success Tip
Pre-record a selection of music of varying tempos to make the activity move more quickly.

Procedures

Level 1   Turn off the lights in the room. Shine the spotlight, flashlight, or projector light onto the wall. Invite the child to stand between the light and the wall. Talk about his shadow. Help the child discover his shadow moves when he moves. Start the music and encourage the child to move to the music. If the child is reluctant to move, offer suggestions like, "Raise your arms over your head" or "Shake your whole body." Ask the child to make his shadow move as he moves.

Level 2   Shine the spotlight, flashlight, or projector light onto the wall. Start the music. Encourage the child to move to the music. Ask the child to watch his shadow move. Then play fast music. Use the word *fast* to talk about the music. Encourage the child to change his dancing to fit the music. Describe what he's doing and talk about the change in movement of his shadow. Then play slow music. Use the word *slow* to talk about the music. Encourage the child to change his dancing to fit the slow music. Describe what he's doing and talk about the change in movement of his shadow. Continue dancing to music of varying tempos.

Level 3   Cover the wall with sheets of white paper. Shine the spotlight, flashlight, or projector light onto the wall. Start the music. Encourage the child to move to the music. Ask the child to watch his shadow move. Then add an additional direction. Ask the child to stop moving when he hears the music stop and to hold his pose. When the child understands the task, trace his shadow on the paper-covered wall as he poses. Have the child dance and pose until you've traced several shadows.

Movement
For Parents & Professionals: Preschool

Then look at the traced poses. Point to different body parts and talk about their positions. Have the child try to fit his shadow back into a traced pose.

Dialogue Highlights

Talk about what you are doing. Here are some examples.

Level 1

- *Look at the bright light.*
- *Walk in front of the light.*
- *What do you see on the wall?*
- *You see your shadow.*
- *Can you make your shadow move?*
- *When you move, your shadow moves.*
- *Make it move again.*

Level 2

- *I'll play some music.*
- *Let's make our shadows move to the music.*
- *Listen to the slow music.*
- *It makes me move slowly. You move slowly too.*
- *Watch how your shadow moves.*
- *Now let's move fast.*

Level 3

- *Now it's time to make a picture of your shadow.*
- *When the music stops, you stop too.*
- *Try to stand still until I say you can move.*
- *Good, you stopped moving! Now I can trace your shadow.*
- *Try to stay very still.*
- *Okay, you can move.*
- *I can still see your shape.*
- *I traced your shadow on the wall.*
- *There's your arm. It's over your head.*
- *Can you make your shadow fit back in the lines?*

Extension Activity

Materials: bright light; various items like a fork, pair of scissors, stuffed bear

Play a shadow guessing game. Collect various items. Take turns holding the things between the light and the wall. Look at the shadow and try to guess what it is.

Promoting Peer Interaction

Materials: bright light, a blank wall, large sheets of white paper, tape, wide-tipped marker

Have two children stand next to each other, facing the wall, so you can see their shadows. Have them put their shadows together to make a "creature." Let the children direct each other how to move to complete the creature. Have them hold their pose. Quickly trace the shadow on the paper-covered wall. Encourage the children to talk about their creature.

Work It Out

Skills
- gross motor imitation
- following directions

Materials
- tape player or CD player
- tape or CD with music that varies in tempo
- the child's own gym shoes or rubber-soled shoes
- pair of large tube socks (optional)
- scissors (optional)

Levels 2 & 3
- *Work It Out* chart, page 87
- wide-tipped marker

Success Tips

Help children learn to drink water as part of physical activity. Plan a water break during this activity.

If the child has a physical disability or health concern, you may need to modify this activity. Consult with the child's doctor or physical therapist.

Procedures

For an inexpensive pair of leg warmers, cut off the feet from a pair of tube socks. Have the child put on his leg warmers and gym shoes. Be ready to help the child if he can't dress alone. Take the child into an open space and start the music.

Level 1   Demonstrate simple stretches like touching your toes, stretching to the side, or twisting. Help the child do the stretches you've modeled. Count aloud with the music as you do four to six repetitions of each stretch.

Level 2   Help the child do four to six repetitions of simple stretches like touching your toes, stretching to the side, or twisting. Show the child the *Work It Out* chart. Point to the first exercise figure and demonstrate that exercise. Have the child try the exercise. Continue for all four exercises pictured on the chart. Practice until the child is familiar with each exercise. Then turn on the music. Complete four to six repetitions of each exercise in the order listed on the chart. Keep track of how many repetitions you and the child can do.

Level 3   Follow Level 2. Then have the child lead you through the exercise routine. Help only as needed.

Dialogue Highlights	Talk about what you are doing. Here are some examples.

Level 1

- *Let's exercise!*
- *First put on your leg warmers.*
- *I hold my leg warmer in two hands.*
- *I put my foot in. Now I pull. You try it.*
- *I can tell you're ready to exercise!*
- *Let's stand up.*
- *First we reach up high. Then we reach down low.*
- *Let's do it again.*
- *Reach up high. Reach down low.*
- *Nice stretching!*

Level 2

- *Here's an exercise chart.*
- *This means jumping jacks.*
- *Watch me do jumping jacks.*
- *Now you do jumping jacks.*
- *This picture means sit-up.*
- *Good, now you know all the exercises.*
- *We're ready to begin.*
- *I'll start the music.*
- *Let's do four jumping jacks.*
- *One, two, three, four. Good!*

Level 3

- *Great, you know all the exercises.*
- *Now you be the leader.*
- *Good, you remembered to turn on the music.*
- *That's right, stretches are first.*

Extension Activity	Let the child help you plan a new exercise routine. Have the child perform his routine for friends, relatives, or neighbors.
Promoting Peer Interaction	Ask the child to teach the exercise routine to another child.

Work It Out Chart

jumping jacks

_____

_____

arm circles

_____

_____

sit-ups

_____

_____

leg lifts

_____

_____

Leaping Lizards!

Skills
- jumping with both feet
- using the direction words *down*, *up*, and *jump*

Materials
- tape player or CD player
- tape or CD of music with a strong, steady beat

Level 2
- sturdy step stool 4" to 6" high or the bottom step of a flight of stairs

Success Tip
Teach jumping skills on a carpeted surface to minimize slipping or injury.

Procedures

Level 1   Help the child experience the motion of jumping. Have the child stand beside you. Say the word *down* and bend your knees. Then say the word *up* and straighten your knees. Ask the child to copy you as you go down and up. Help the child by placing your hands around his waist and gently guiding him down and up. Continue to practice until the child bends and straightens his knees when you say the words *down* and *up*.

Now show the child how to jump. Bend your knees. Then immediately straighten them and jump. Ask the child to bend and jump with you. Tandem jumping may help the child learn to jump. To tandem jump, stand behind the child, press your knees against his body, and put your hands around his waist for support. Say the word *down* as you and the child bend your knees. Wait until the child straightens his legs. Then say the word *up* and lift him off the floor. Finish the activity by playing music. Encourage the child to jump with the music.

Level 2   Many children can make the down and up jumping movement, but still can't get airborne. Help the child get the feel of jumping. Have the child stand on the stool. Hold the child's hands. Then ask the child to bend his knees (go down) and jump up and off the stool. If you find that you're pulling the child off the stool, move your hands to the child's waist. This way you can support the child without pulling him off the stool. Your support and the pull of gravity may be all he needs to jump. Finish the activity by playing music. Encourage the child to jump with the music.

Level 3   Teach the child to jump consecutively. First bend your knees and jump. Make three consecutive jumps while you say, "Jump, jump, jump." Then ask the child to jump, jump, jump. If consecutive jumping is difficult for the child, try using the tandem jumping described in Level 1. Play music to make jumping more fun. As the child becomes skilled at jumping, show him how to jump in time with the music. Talk about the speed of the music. Show the child how to jump quickly during the fast songs and slowly during the slow songs.

Dialogue Highlights

Talk about what you are doing. Here are some examples.

Level 1

- *Today we'll move down and up.*
- *Watch me.*
- *I move down. Then I move up.*
- *Watch my knees.*
- *They bend when I go down. They're straight when I come up.*
- *Let's move down and up.*
- *Now let's jump!*
- *Bend down. Now push up. Try to lift your feet off the floor.*
- *Great! Keep jumping!*

Level 2

- *Let's jump.*
- *Watch me and try to jump.*
- *Down, then up!*
- *Let's try a big jump.*
- *Step up on the stool.*
- *Hold my hands.*
- *Bend your knees and go down.*
- *Now move up and jump.*

Level 3

- *Watch me jump.*
- *I bend my knees and go down. Then I jump up!*
- *I went down and up.*
- *I can jump three times. Jump, jump, jump.*
- *Let's jump, jump, jump together.*
- *Let's put on some jumping music.*
- *Can we jump in time with the music?*

Extension Activity

Materials: a die

Have the child roll a die. Count the dots on the side that lands faceup. Ask the child to jump that number of times. Have the child jump across the room toward a "finish" line.

**Promoting
Peer
Interaction**

Materials: large balloon or ball

Ask two children to face each other. Tell them to put their hands on the other child's elbows. Have the children practice jumping up and down together. Then move 2 – 3 feet away from the children and have them jump to you. Continue practicing until they are able to jump for a distance of ten feet.

Balance a large balloon on their joined arms. Place a container ten feet away from the children. Tell the children to jump together to the container and see if they can drop the balloon into the container.

My, What Big Feet You Have!

Skills
- maintaining balance
- walking heel-to-toe on a line
- using the describing words *cold, squishy, wet,* and *slippery*
- washing and drying
- following directions

Materials
- cookie sheet
- roll of butcher paper, newsprint, or freezer paper
- any washable paint
- washtub filled with warm, soapy water
- washcloth and towel
- two small chairs
- scissors

Level 3
- tape
- marker
- another cookie sheet

Success Tips

Some children may be hesitant to put their feet or hands in paint. They may be more willing to participate if the adult goes first.

When making water footprints outside in the Extension Activity/Peer Interaction, try to find a shaded area so the footprints remain visible longer.

Procedures

Spread a thin layer of paint onto the cookie sheet. Put the cookie sheet on the floor in front of a small chair.

Using familiar materials in a different way promotes creativity.

Level 1 Cut a small sheet of paper from the roll and put it next to the cookie sheet. Place the washtub, washcloth, and towel close to the work area.

Ask the child to put his hands into the paint. Encourage the child to wiggle his fingers. Use describing words like *cold, squishy, wet* and *slippery* to talk about the paint. Allow the child enough time to adjust to the feel of the paint and to experiment with moving his hands through the paint. Then have the child hold his hands up, palms forward. Remove the cookie sheet and put the sheet of paper in front of the chair. Help the child lean forward and place his hands on the paper. Gently apply pressure over the child's hands and fingers to make a complete hand print. Ask the child to carefully lift his hands. Remove the painted paper and place the washtub in front of the child. Help the child wash and dry his hands.

Level 2 Unroll six feet of paper on the floor in front of the cookie sheet. Place one chair by the cookie sheet and the other chair at the other end of the unrolled paper. Put the washtub, washcloth, and towel next to the second chair. Ask the child to take off his shoes and socks and to roll up his pant legs. Have the child sit in the small chair by the paint. Help the child put his feet into the paint. Encourage the child to wiggle his toes. Use describing words like *cold, squishy, wet,* and *slippery* to talk about the paint. Allow the child enough time to adjust to the feel of the paint and to experiment with moving his feet through the paint.

Then help the child stand up. Encourage the child to hold his arms out to the side to keep his balance. If the child can't maintain his balance, hold his hand or put your hands around his waist to support him as he walks across the paper. Then help the child sit in the chair at the end of the paper. Help the child wash and dry his feet. Be sure to check for paint between the toes! If needed, help the child put on his shoes and socks. Let the painted footprints dry completely. Then ask the child to walk across the paper, matching his steps to the painted footprints.

Level 3 Introduce the child to foot painting with the Level 2 activity. Unroll two six-foot lengths of paper. Tape the lengths side by side. Help the child plan and draw the outline of a large, simple object like a circle, hand, or car on the paper. Have the child walk along the outline of the object.

Then have the child walk along the outline of the object with paint on his feet. Reapply paint onto the child's feet as needed. When the outline of the object is complete, have the child add details in a second color (facial features in the circle, fingernails on the hand, or doors on the car).

Dialogue Highlights Talk about what you are doing. Here are some examples.

Level 1
- *Here's some paint.*
- *Here's some paper.*
- *Today we'll paint with our hands.*
- *Put your hands in the paint.*
- *Yes, the paint is cold (squishy, wet, slippery).*
- *Now pick up your hands.*
- *Put them on the paper. I'll help you press down.*
- *Pick up your hands again.*
- *You made a handprint!*
- *Let's wash your hands.*

Level 2
- *Yes, you get to paint with your feet!*
- *Put your feet in the paint.*
- *Move them around.*
- *It's slippery!*
- *Now stand up. I'll hold your hand.*
- *Take a step. Walk across the paper.*
- *Look at your footprints!*
- *Sit in the chair.*
- *Put your feet in the tub.*
- *I'll help you wash your feet.*

Level 3
- *Let's make a big picture.*
- *What should we make?*
- *Yes, let's make a car.*
- *You drew a big car.*
- *Now you're going to trace the car with paint on your feet.*
- *Put paint on your feet.*
- *Put one foot here. Now put your other foot in front of this foot.*
- *Keep your feet close together.*
- *Try to stay on the line.*
- *You're almost out of paint on your feet.*
- *Here's the paint tray.*
- *Hold my hands and put your feet into the paint.*
- *You went around the whole car.*
- *Sit in the chair and wash your feet.*
- *What else does this car need? Doors.*
- *Let's use red paint to make the doors.*

Extension Activity

Materials: washtub, outdoor cement surface

Fill the washtub with warm water and place on an outdoor cement surface. Have the child remove his shoes and socks and step into the water. Have the child step out of the water and onto the cement. Ask the child to follow you as you walk a short distance. Look at the pattern of the child's footprints. Demonstrate different ways of walking like walking with your toes pointing in or walking with your heels pointing in. Compare the footprints.

My, What Big Feet You Have!, *continued*

Promoting Peer Interaction

Materials: washtub, outdoor cement surface

Fill the washtub with warm water. Make footprints with water on an outside cement surface. Have one child start making "water" footprints. Ask a second child to follow the first child's footprints. Have them look at the patterns their footprints made. For more fun, create unique footprints. Have each child walk in a line using a different walk, like walking on tiptoe and walking with toes turned out.

Conquer the Mountain

Skills
- climbing stairs (holding on, without holding on, carrying an object)
- following directions
- using action words
- using location words

Materials
- flight of stairs with a railing or wall on both sides
- direction game cards, pages 109 – 111

Level 3
- beanbag or beanbag-sized stuffed animal

Success Tips

Clear the stairs before beginning this activity.

Have the child wear rubber-soled shoes to keep from slipping on a step.

Make two copies of each sheet of direction game cards so there can be a set for each player.

Procedures

Practice walking up and down a flight of stairs with the child to be sure he has the balance to safely complete this activity. Talk about stair-climbing safety. You might tell the child, "Step on one step at a time," "Watch where you're going," and "Hang on to the railing or wall."

Level 1   Copy and cut out the direction game cards on page 109. Stand at the bottom of the flight of stairs with the child, one of you to the right and one to the left. Choose a direction game card. Read the direction and follow it. Then have the child choose a direction game card. Read the card to the child and help him follow it. Continue the game until one of you reaches the top of the staircase.

Level 2   Copy and cut out the direction game cards on page 110. Mix them in with the cards from Level 1. Play the game as described in Level 1.

Level 3   Copy and cut out the direction game cards on page 111. Add these cards to the cards from Levels 1 and 2. Have the child climb up the middle of the staircase while following the directions on the game cards. Play the game as described in Level 1. (Note: The child will carry the beanbag for some of the directions, putting it down and picking it up as needed.)

Dialogue Highlights	Talk about what you are doing. Here are some examples.

Level 1

- *Here are the stairs.*
- *Let's go up.*
- *Good! You put your hand on the railing.*
- *Now we'll use the stairs to play a game.*
- *You stand on this side of the staircase. I'll stand on this side.*
- *First I'll take a card.*
- *It says to go up one step. I'll go up one step.*
- *Now you take a card.*
- *It says to go up two steps. One, two.*
- *My turn again.*

Level 2

- *We'll use the stairs to play a game.*
- *Remember to step on one step at a time and watch where you're going.*
- *I'll take a card.*
- *My card says to go up three steps. One, two, three.*
- *I went up three steps.*
- *Now you choose a card.*
- *Your card says to go up one step.*

Level 3

- *Let's play again. This time we'll use a beanbag.*
- *Carry the beanbag up the stairs.*
- *Take a card.*
- *Your card says to go up two steps with a beanbag.*
- *Hold the beanbag.*

Extension Activity

Materials: construction paper, colored markers

Put different colored sheets of paper, or paper with numbers on it, on each step. Have the child follow your directions as he climbs. For example, you might have him climb to the red step or to the step with the number 2.

Promoting Peer Interaction

Use the direction cards from the Level 2 and Level 3 games. Show the children how to "read" the direction cards using the symbols. Practice until the children understand this task. Then give each child half of the direction cards. Have the first child choose a card and tell the second child what he is to do. Continue the game until all direction cards have been "read."

It's in the Can

Skills
- throwing a ball
- using action and location words
- improving hand-eye coordination
- identifying numbers
- counting

Materials
- wastebasket with a 12" to 18" diameter opening
- piece of oak tag large enough to cover the wastebasket
- colored markers
- scissors
- masking tape
- 4" to 6" soft ball or a beanbag

Level 3
- containers of varying sizes with 8" to 12" diameter openings

---

Success Tip

Some children are afraid of clowns. For these children, just draw a funny face or the face of an animal.

Procedures

Level 1 Draw a clown face on the oak tag with a mouth large enough for the ball or beanbag to easily pass through. Cut out the mouth to create an opening. Place the oak tag across the top of the wastebasket and tape one edge of the oak tag to the wastebasket to create a hinge. Show the child the clown's face and describe its features. Explain to the child that it's time to feed the clown. Show him how to drop the ball through the clown's mouth into the wastebasket. Help the child aim the ball to "feed" the clown. Have the child retrieve the ball.

Level 2 When the child can easily feed the clown as described in Level 1, remove the clown's face. Put the wastebasket next to a wall. Place a line of masking tape approximately three feet from the front of the wastebasket. Tell the child that it's time to play basketball. Show the child how to throw the ball into the wastebasket. Help the child aim and throw the ball into the wastebasket as needed. As the child masters throwing the ball into the wastebasket, show him the masking tape line. Encourage him to throw the ball from behind the line. Continue to practice until the child consistently throws the ball into the wastebasket.

Level 3 Introduce the child to basketball with the Level 2 activity. Then challenge the child by placing several different-sized containers next to the wall. Give the child time to practice throwing the ball into the containers. Assign a point value to each container. Make the larger containers worth one point and the smaller containers worth three points. Tally the number of points the child earns after taking five shots with the ball.

Dialogue Highlights

Talk about what you are doing. Here are some examples.

Level 1

- *Let's play a game.*
- *Look! I made a clown.*
- *He has silly eyes. (He has a red nose. He has a big mouth.)*
- *The clown is hungry!*
- *We need to feed him.*
- *I'll feed him this ball.*
- *Do you want to feed the clown?*
- *Here's the ball.*
- *Feed the clown.*
- *Hold the ball above his mouth. Now drop the ball.*
- *Good, you fed the clown!*

Level 2

- *We're going to play another game.*
- *Watch. I'll throw the ball into the wastebasket.*
- *It went in!*
- *Do you want a turn?*
- *You got the ball in the basket!*
- *Now let's throw the ball from behind this line.*
- *Do you think you can do it from here?*

Level 3

- *Now I have some other baskets for our game.*
- *These baskets are smaller.*
- *Do you think you can throw the ball into them?*
- *I'll put them by the wall.*
- *I'll stand by the line and throw the ball. I made it!*
- *Do you want to try?*
- *You remembered to put your toes on the line.*
- *Aim for the can. You made it!*
- *Let's try another one.*

Extension Activity

Materials: laundry basket, pair of socks

Play laundry basketball. Use a pair of rolled-up socks as a ball. Have the child stand in front of a laundry basket and throw the rolled-up socks into it. After the child makes the basket, have him take one step back and shoot again. See how many baskets the child can make in a row.

Promoting Peer Interaction

Materials: soft ball

Have two children stand back to back. Ask the children to take three steps forward. Then have the children turn and face each other. Give one child a soft ball (Nerf® ball). Have the other child form a hoop with his arms. Tell the child with the ball to try to throw the ball through the other child's arms. Tell the child forming the hoop that he can move his arms to help the other child make a basket. Have the children take turns throwing the ball. After each child makes a basket, have the children move one step further apart.

Balloons Anyone?

Skills

- catching
- throwing
- responding to signals
- using action words

Materials

- several 8" to 10" balloons

Level 3

- water

Success Tips

If the child is tempted to put things in his mouth, put the balloon into a nylon net or panty hose and tie each end. If the balloon pops, the pieces are contained.

When playing with the water balloons, periodically tell the child how many water balloons are left. When the last water balloon is being used, remind the child that the activity will end when that balloon breaks.

Store prepared water balloons in a container of water to minimize breakage.

Procedures

Level 1

Blow up a balloon. Show the child how to catch. First hold your arms out. Then bring your arms close to your body as if you're catching something or clasping your hands to your chest. Help the child practice this catching movement.

Now add the balloon to the activity. Have the child hold out his arms and then bring them close to his body. When he brings in his arms, put a balloon in his arms and say, "Catch." Continue saying, "Catch," and putting the balloon into his arms until he brings his arms in on cue. Then stand two feet away from the child. Say the child's name to make sure he's ready. Gently throw the balloon to the child. Say, "Catch," to cue the child to bring his arms in to catch the balloon. Continue practicing until the child can easily catch the balloon.

Level 2

When the child can easily catch the balloon, he's ready to play a game of "Catch." Stand three to four feet away from the child. Say the child's name to make sure he's ready. Use an underhand toss to throw the balloon to the child. Then have the child throw the balloon to you. Prompt the child to say your name to make sure you're ready. Have the child use an underhand toss to throw the balloon to you. When the child can easily throw and catch the balloon from this distance, move farther apart.

Level 3 When the child can easily play catch, it's time for more fun and challenge! Follow the activity as described in Level 2, but use water balloons outside. Have the child see how long he can keep the water balloon from breaking. Stand three feet apart for the first throw. After each catch, each player takes one step backward. Count the number of catches before the balloon breaks.

Dialogue Highlights Talk about what you are doing. Here are some examples.

Level 1
- *Hold your arms out.*
- *Now bring them in.*
- *Give yourself a hug!*
- *Let's do it again. Arms out. Bring them in.*
- *Now we're ready to play catch.*
- *Hold out your arms.*
- *Here comes the balloon.*
- *Bring your arms in.*
- *Catch! You caught the balloon!*

Level 2
- *I'll throw the balloon to you.*
- *You catch the balloon, then throw it to me.*
- *Here comes the balloon. Good catch!*
- *Now call my name. Okay, I'm ready!*
- *Throw the balloon.*
- *I caught it!*

Level 3
- *Now we're going to play with balloons that have water in them.*
- *Be ready to catch the balloon or you might get wet!*
- *Now take a step backward and throw the balloon to me.*
- *I caught it!*

Extension Activity Materials: soft foam ball or beach ball

When the child has mastered throwing and catching a balloon, play catch with a soft foam ball or beach ball.

**Promoting
Peer
Interaction**

Materials: water balloons

On a warm day, have a water balloon relay outdoors. Have the children stand in a line. Space the children three feet apart. Give a water balloon to the first child in line. Tell the child to face the second child and toss the balloon to him. The second child then faces the third child and throws the balloon to him. Have the children continue tossing the balloon to each other until the last child in line has it. Then have the last child run to the front of the line to begin the relay again. Count the number of times the children throw the balloon before it drops or breaks.

102

Movement
For Parents & Professionals: Preschool

Join the PBA
(Preschool Bowlers Association)

Skills
- rolling a ball toward a target
- using action words
- learning game-playing skills
- taking turns

Materials
- large ball
- empty two-liter plastic soft drink bottle
- sand or water
- timer

Levels 2 & 3
- 5 additional empty two-liter plastic soft drink bottles
- masking tape

Success Tips
When playing the bowling game in Level 3, mark the center of the circle with masking tape on the floor. The tape will remind the child where to stand.

Put 3" to 4" of sand or water in the bottom of each soft drink bottle to make it more of a challenge to knock over.

Procedures

Level 1   Have the child sit on the floor. Sit across from the child. Show the child how to sit with his legs straight out and spread apart. Roll the ball to the child. As you roll the ball say, "Push." When the child catches the ball, ask him to push it back to you. If the child needs help pushing the ball, sit behind him and put your hands over his. When the child can easily roll a ball, he's ready for bowling.

Put one bottle in an open area. Have the child sit 6' from the bottle. Ask the child to watch you roll the ball toward the bottle and knock it over. Then let the child roll the ball and knock over the bottle. When the child knocks over the bottle, have him set it up again. Set the timer. See how many times the child can knock the "pin" down before the timer rings.

Level 2   Begin the activity as described in Level 1. When the child can easily knock down one bottle, set up six bottles in rows of one, two, and three (like bowling pins at a bowling alley). Make a starting line with masking tape 8' to 10' from the first pin. Have the child watch you roll the ball and knock over the "pins." Then show the child how to push the ball on the floor. Encourage him to practice. After several practice rolls, have a game of bowling. Give the child two chances to roll the ball. Then count the number of pins knocked down. Have the child reset his pins.

Level 3　　When the child can easily knock down the bowling pins, change the game. Put a bottle 6' behind the child. Help the child roll the ball backward through his legs to knock the pin down. Have the child practice until he can easily knock down the pin. Then arrange the bottles in a large circle. Have the child stand in the middle of the circle, with his feet 1' apart. Tell him that he can't move his feet. Have him roll the ball forward and backward to knock down all the pins.

Dialogue Highlights　　Talk about what you are doing. Here are some examples.

Level 1
- *Sit on the floor like this.*
- *Watch me push the ball.*
- *Now you push the ball.*
- *Now we're ready to play a game.*
- *Here's a bowling pin.*
- *Push the ball at the bowling pin.*
- *Try to knock it down.*
- *You knocked down the pin.*
- *Please put the pin back up.*
- *I'll set the timer.*
- *See how many times you can knock down the pin before the timer rings.*

Level 2
- *Look at this line.*
- *Your feet can't go over the line.*
- *Watch me roll the ball.*
- *Can you show me how to roll the ball?*
- *Roll the ball toward the pins.*
- *You knocked down two pins. Good job!*
- *Take another turn.*
- *See if you can knock down the rest of the pins!*
- *How many did you knock down?*

Level 3
- *Watch me! I'm going to be silly and bowl backward.*
- *I turn around and stand with my feet apart.*
- *Then I bend over and look for the pin.*
- *Now I roll the ball backward through my legs.*
- *Did I knock it down?*
- *Your turn.*

- *Let's play another silly bowling game.*
- *I'll put the bowling pins in a big circle.*
- *Stand in the middle of the circle. Don't move your feet.*
- *See how many pins you can knock down with the ball.*
- *You can bowl backward to knock over the pins.*

Extension Activity

Materials: ball, 2 or 3 different-sized hoops
(Note: Wooden embroidery hoops are relatively inexpensive and are available in a variety of sizes.)

Hold the largest hoop several feet from the child. Rest the bottom of the hoop on the floor. Have the child roll the ball through the hoop. Repeat the activity using the next smaller hoop. Then hold the hoops 3' to 4' apart, one behind the other. Let the child try to roll the ball so it goes through both hoops.

Promoting Peer Interaction

Arrange the bottle bowling pins in a line, placing them 3' apart. Have the children stand facing each other, one on either side of the first pin. Give the ball to one child. Have the first child roll the ball to the second child, going between the first and second pins. Have the second child roll the ball back to the first child, going between the second and third pins. Have the children continue rolling the ball back and forth between the pins. Challenge the children to roll the ball without knocking any pins over. You can also have the children stand farther away from the pins or take a step backward each time they roll the ball to each other.

What a Kick!

Skills
- kicking
- using action words

Materials
- 10" to 12" playground ball
- 2 small chairs

Level 3
- large box
- scissors
- marker

Success Tip

In Level 3, place a weight like a heavy book on the top of the box to prevent it from moving.

Procedures

Level 1   Have the child sit in a chair. Sit across from him. Tell the child you'll kick the ball to him. Ask the child to kick the ball back to you. Gently kick the ball toward the child. If the child needs help to kick the ball back, put the ball in front of his foot. Then move his foot forward and say, "Kick." When the child can kick the ball, move outside. Set up chairs next to each other or sit on some steps. Have a contest to see who can kick the ball the farthest.

Level 2   Modify the above activity by having the child stand up to kick the ball. First have the child stand beside his chair. Encourage him to hold onto the chair back for balance. Roll the ball to the child. If it's hard for the child to kick the moving ball, put the ball in front of him without rolling it. When the child can kick the ball, move farther away and roll the ball to him. Encourage the child to loosen his hold on the chair. Have him use two fingers to hold on and then completely let go. Show the child how to hold his arms out to his sides for balance when he kicks. Then stand next to the child. Have a contest to see who can kick the ball the farthest.

> *When taking turns during an activity with a child, be sure to model making and recovering from mistakes. This allows the child to learn strategies for correcting mistakes, persist with a task, develop alternate strategies, and develop problem-solving skills.*

Level 3   Cut openings on three sides of a box. Make
the first opening in the box slightly larger
than the ball. Make the second opening in the
box 3" larger than the first opening. Make the
third opening in the box 6" larger than the
first opening. Write the number 5 above the
smallest opening, the number 3 above the
medium-sized opening, and the number 1
above the largest opening. These numbers
indicate the number of points scored when a
ball rolls into the opening.

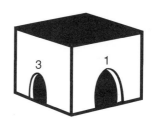

When the child has learned how to kick a ball, he's ready to kick
toward a target. Put the box with the largest opening 10' across from
where the child will kick the ball. Have the child watch you kick the
ball toward the box. Show the child how to kick with his feet straight
forward and how to aim for the opening. When the child can kick the
ball through the large hole, let him aim for the smaller holes. After
the child practices kicking the ball through the holes, play a game.
Take three turns kicking the ball toward each opening on the box.
Keep track of how many points you earn.

Dialogue   Talk about what you are doing. Here are some examples.
Highlights

Level 1
- *Get ready to kick.*
- *Here comes the ball.*
- *Kick it!*
- *Let's go outside.*
- *Sit here on the step.*
- *I'll sit by you.*
- *Here's the ball.*
- *Kick it!*
- *It hit the tree.*
- *Go get the ball.*
- *Now it's my turn.*

Level 2
- *Stand beside your chair.*
- *Hold on to the back of your chair with one hand.*
- *I'll roll the ball.*
- *When it comes to you, kick it.*
- *Here comes the ball.*
- *Good kick!*
- *Now hold on to your chair with only two fingers.*

Level 3
- *Look at the hole in this box.*
- *Can you kick the ball through the hole?*
- *Now look at the numbers on the box.*
- *These numbers are the points for a game.*
- *If you kick the ball into the hole with the five over it, you get five points.*
- *How many points do you get for kicking the ball through this hole?*
- *Let's see how many points we can get.*

Extension Activity

Materials: box, large can, paper grocery bag

Set up three objects like a box, a large can, and a paper grocery bag at the end of a play area. Tell the child to kick the ball and try to hit one of the objects. Then ask the child to kick the ball at a specific object. For more fun, have the child move farther away each time he kicks the ball.

Promoting Peer Interaction

Materials: small chairs (one per child), ball, timer

Play a variation of the game *Hot Potato* using a small chair for each child and one ball. Arrange the small chairs in a circle facing the center. Tell the children to quickly kick the ball away when it comes to them. Set a timer and play until it rings. The child closest to the ball when the timer rings gets to put the ball away. Encourage the children to keep the ball within the circle of chairs.

108

Movement
For Parents & Professionals: Preschool

Game Cards for Conquer the Mountain

Copy and cut apart these cards for the activities on pages 95 – 96.

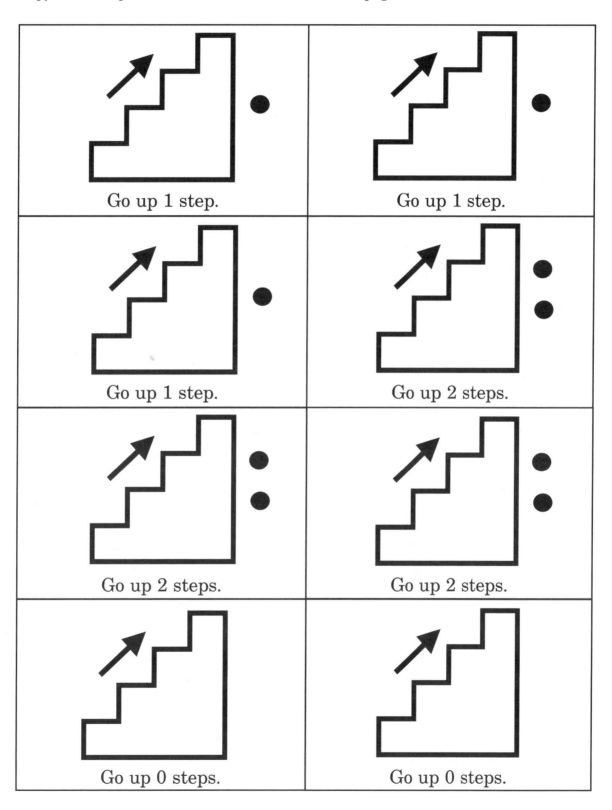

Game Cards for Conquer the Mountain, *continued*

Copy and cut apart these cards for the activities on pages 95 – 96.

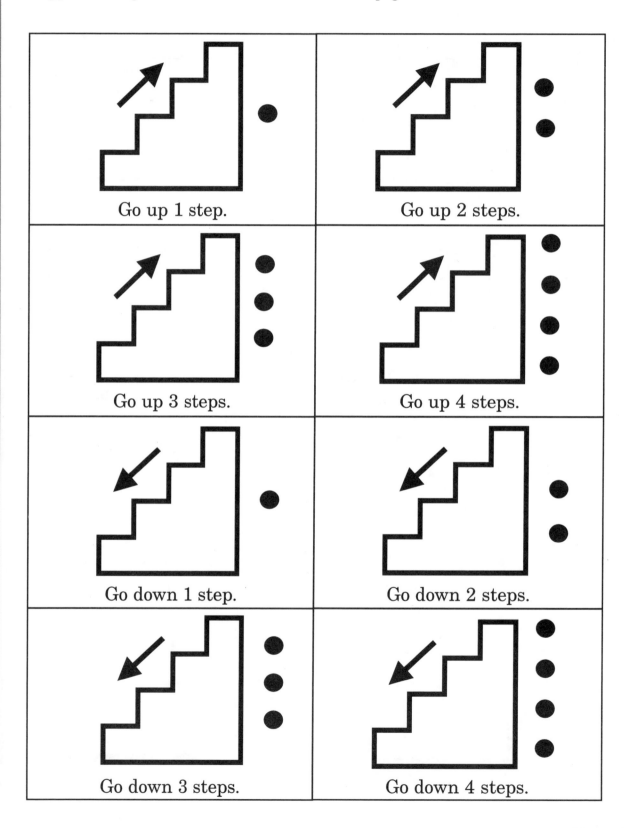

Go up 1 step.

Go up 2 steps.

Go up 3 steps.

Go up 4 steps.

Go down 1 step.

Go down 2 steps.

Go down 3 steps.

Go down 4 steps.

Movement
For Parents & Professionals: Preschool

Game Cards for Conquer the Mountain, *continued*

Copy and cut apart these cards for the activities on pages 95 – 96.

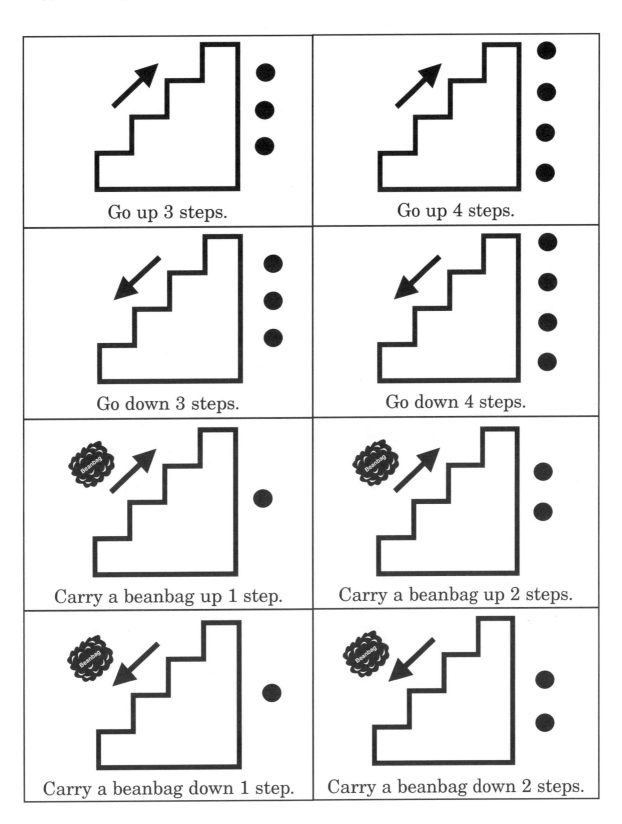

Go up 3 steps.

Go up 4 steps.

Go down 3 steps.

Go down 4 steps.

Carry a beanbag up 1 step.

Carry a beanbag up 2 steps.

Carry a beanbag down 1 step.

Carry a beanbag down 2 steps.

Strategies for Learning Through Daily Routines

> "Because of children's short attention spans, one may tend to think that children need an infinite number of choices and new surprises every day. Children actually crave routine, repetition, and consistency."[1]

Becoming independent in self-help skills is a major goal of the preschool years. Skills like dressing or grooming are part of daily activities for all of us. It is essential to provide guidance, support, and time for practice for the child throughout the day to develop the child's self-help skills.

In addition to activities to teach self-help skills, the activities in this section include turning routine daily activities into opportunities for learning.

When teaching self-help skills, assess the child's current skill level. Consider which skills the child can complete independently and which require adult assistance to complete. Assistance can be provided for most self-help tasks by *backward chaining*. Backward chaining occurs when an adult provides assistance with an activity until the last step, which the child completes independently. For example, when eating with a spoon, the adult holds her hand over the child's and guides the child to fill the spoon, bring it to her mouth, put it in her mouth, and remove it. The child independently lowers the spoon to the bowl. When the child is able to complete that step independently, the adult provides assistance until the last two steps. The adult continues to provide less and less support as the child's skill increases. In order to use backward chaining successfully, the skill must first be broken into steps. Use a key word or phrase at each step of the task that can later serve as a prompt to the child as she works to complete the task independently.

To promote independence in the bathroom:

- store toothbrush, toothpaste, combs, and brushes in a drawer that is easily accessible or in a container on the counter.

- use a push-button toothpaste dispenser.

- provide a stool for the child to stand on at the sink or toilet.

- place a sticker on the faucet for cold water to distinguish between hot and cold.

- use a pump soap dispenser for easier hand-washing.

[1]Ford, 1993.

- have a towel bar or paper towel dispenser at the child's level.

- use a wide-toothed comb or brush. Take turns when styling hair (adult brushes out snarls and establishes the part, child combs through). "No-fuss" hair styles make grooming tasks easier.

- use a bath mitt rather than a washcloth. It stays on the child's hand more easily for bathing.

- use swim goggles to keep soap and water out of the child's eyes when shampooing.

To promote independence in dressing:

- select clothes that have large zippers and buttons, Velcro® fasteners, elastic waistbands, large neck openings, and designs to distinguish front from back.

- choose a time to practice when you're not rushed. If your morning routine doesn't allow adequate time for practice, practice at night while undressing for bath and putting on pajamas. Weekend mornings may be another good time for dressing practice. You can also practice with dress-up clothes during playtime.

- it may be easier to assist the child with dressing if you sit or stand behind her.

- take turns with dressing tasks. The child may be more cooperative if you put on one sock and she puts on the other.

- provide hooks or pegs at the child's level to encourage hanging up coats. Store hats, mittens, and scarves in a container on the floor by the coats.

- store the child's everyday clothes in the bottom drawers. Hang the child's clothes on a low bar in the closet.

- at bedtime, select and lay out clothes for the next day.

To promote independence at mealtimes:

- have child-sized dishes and utensils available.

- use a booster seat as needed to seat the child at an appropriate height at the table.

- serve sticky foods like applesauce, yogurt, or pudding when the child is learning to use a spoon.

- serve chunks of soft food like fruits or vegetables that are easy to spear when the child is learning to use a fork.

- practice cutting skills with foods like canned fruits, chunks of cheese, or toast. Be sure to use an appropriate-sized knife (a plastic knife may work well) and supervise carefully. It is also fun to practice cutting play dough with a knife.

To promote independence with household tasks:

- use spray and wipe cleaners that make it easy for the child to help. The child can clean countertops, the front of the refrigerator, windows, and mirrors.

- a feather duster can be a fun way for a child to help with dusting.

- when doing laundry, the child can help match socks or fold small towels and washcloths. The child may enjoy transferring clothes from the washer to the dryer or from the dryer to a laundry basket. It's also fun to put in the laundry soap and/or dryer sheet.

- in the kitchen, the child can help stir during meal preparations.

- a place mat with the outline of dishes and utensils makes it easier for the child to learn to set the table.

- a sink full of soapy water and plastic bowls and cups may entertain the child while you work on another task.

In addition to learning self-help skills, a daily routine is important to the preschool child because it provides consistency and predictability. The child can develop responsibility by participating in a regular routine. She can take care of her own needs as well as establish herself as a helper in the family.

Cooking and Food Preparation

Cooking and food preparation with children can be a very enjoyable experience. Activities involving cooking and food help children develop physical skills as well as develop language concepts, daily living, and cognitive skills. Begin with simple tasks like tearing lettuce before introducing more difficult tasks like cracking an egg. The easiest food preparation skills require the use of the child's whole hand and arm, like dipping a carrot into a dip. Then the child is ready to progress to tasks requiring more hand-eye coordination, like pouring liquids or spreading butter on bread. Tasks that require coordinating the use of both hands are even more challenging. These tasks might include peeling eggs or kneading dough. The most difficult task for children requires them to work against the resistance of a solid object, like using a knife to cut cheese.

Two-year-olds are generally able to pour, stir, shake, dip, scrub, tear, spread, and roll. Three-year-olds can beat with an eggbeater and grind with a food grinder. Four-year-olds can peel with a scraper and grate with a hand grater.

Here are some suggested ways to involve children in food and meal preparation.

Wash the table.

Help set the table.

Pass the napkins.

Pass the food.

Serve themselves.

Clear their plates from the table.

Pour milk or juice.

Scrub vegetables with brushes.

Dip vegetables in a dip.

Break or tear lettuce.

Place toppings on pizza and snacks.

Add decorations to cookies.

Grease baking pans.

Peel carrots with a scraper.

Wash silverware.

Cut fruits, vegetables, or cheese with supervision and assistance.

Peel fruits and eggs with fingers.

Spread bread with butter or peanut butter.

Shape cookie dough into balls.

Squeeze juice from oranges.

Mash egg yolks for deviled eggs.

Arrange cookies, fruits, or finger foods on a plate.

Crack and separate egg white from egg yolk.

Measure rice, water, or sugar for recipes.

Beat eggs with a fork or eggbeater.

Grind apples with a food grinder.

Add pre-measured ingredients to food.

Shake coconut with food coloring in a jar.

Knead bread dough.

Developmental Sequences for Self-Help Skills

Eating	Grooming	Dressing
o uses spoon to feed self	o rinses and tries to dry hands	o pulls off socks and shoes, laces may be loosened
o drinks from a cup using both hands to hold the cup	o allows teeth to be brushed	o removes loose-fitting, unfastened coat independently
o eats independently, using a spoon and cup with few spills	o washes and dries hands with verbal assistance only	o unzips large zipper
o uses a straw	o brushes teeth with assistance	o removes all unfastened clothing
o drinks from a cup using one hand to hold the cup	o washes face with assistance in drying	o puts on coat or other simple garments
o uses a fork	o wipes nose with a tissue	o puts on shoes
o spreads butter with a knife	o washes and dries hands and face independently	o undoes large snaps
o uses the edge of a spoon or fork to cut food	o brushes teeth independently	o buttons large buttons
o uses a knife for cutting	o combs or brushes hair with assistance	o zips zipper
	o bathes with assistance	o unbuttons own clothing
		o pulls pants up and down
		o buttons medium-sized buttons
		o puts on pullover shirt
		o puts on pants
		o puts on socks
		o fastens and unfastens snaps
		o puts shoes on correct feet
		o dresses with minimal assistance

116   *For Parents & Professionals: Preschool*

Tasting Party

Skills
- categorizing
- identifying sweet/sour foods
- recognizing opposites
- matching
- judging another person's reaction

Materials
- mirror
- knife
- 8 paper cups
- napkin
- cup of water
- portions of the following: dill pickles, grapefruit, unsweetened and sweetened Kool-Aid®, lemon juice, bite-sized marshmallows, sweetened cereal

Level 3
- salted foods like popcorn, crackers, pretzels
- unsalted foods like popcorn, crackers, bread, unsweetened cereal (Cheerios®)

Success Tip
Encourage timid children to participate in this activity by giving them a sweet food for their first taste trial.

Procedures

Put small samples of each of the sweet and sour foods into the paper cups. Pour a small cup of water for the child.

Level 1   Tell the child that she will taste different foods. Explain that some things taste sweet like candy and some things taste sour like a pickle. Taste a sweet food and tell the child how it tasted. Ask the child to watch your face. Go through the same process as you taste a sour food.

Then have the child close her eyes and taste a small sample of a sweet food. Describe her reaction by saying things like, "You're smiling. You must like it," or "Mmm, it must taste good." Tell the child the name of the food and label it "sweet" or "sour." Show the child how to use a napkin to dispose of samples she doesn't like. Offer the child a sip of water after she's tasted a sample.

Level 2   Ask the child what the words *sweet* and *sour* mean. Show the child what happens to your mouth and face when something tastes sweet or sour. Ask the child to copy your "sweet" and "sour" facial expressions.

Invite the child to a special sweet and sour party. Explain she'll taste different foods and decide if they're sweet or sour. Show the child how to use a napkin to dispose of foods she doesn't like. Then ask the child to try the first sample. Have the child close her eyes while you feed her a small sample of food. Have the child open her eyes and watch her face in the mirror. Talk about her reaction when a food sample is sweet and when it is sour. After the child has tasted a food, ask her to guess what she has tasted.

Level 3   Present the activity as described in Level 2. Then present the foods a second time. Have the child sort the food samples by taste. The categories could include salted and unsalted foods or foods that the child likes or dislikes.

Dialogue Highlights   Talk about what you are doing. Here are some examples.

Level 1
- *Today we'll eat and drink some things.*
- *Some things will taste sweet.*
- *Some things will taste sour.*
- *Watch my face.*
- *The pickle made my face pucker like this.*
- *Taste this food.*
- *Look at your face.*

Level 2
- *What are some foods that are sweet? Yes, candy and cake are sweet foods.*
- *What foods are sour?*
- *What do our faces look like when we eat sweet (sour) foods?*
- *Close your eyes and taste.*
- *What food do you think you tasted?*

Level 3
- *Now let's taste the food again.*
- *Let's make two groups. Over here are foods you like. Here are foods you don't like.*
- *Try this food.*
- *Do you like it?*

Extension Activity   Materials: glasses, Kool-Aid®, sugar, spoon

Do a sweet and sour experiment. Mix two glasses of Kool-Aid®, one with sugar and one without. Have the child taste both glasses and talk about how they tasted. Then have the child slowly add sugar to the unsweetened glass of Kool-Aid® to make both glasses taste the same.

118

Daily Routines
For Parents & Professionals: Preschool

Promoting Peer Interaction

Materials: plastic fork, bowl of mixed fruit, cubed cheese, or bite-sized marshmallows

Seat the children next to each other at a small table. Put a bowl of food on the table like mixed fruit, cubed cheese, or bite-sized marshmallows. Ask the first child to pick up a plastic fork, spear a piece of food, and feed the other child. Ask the child to judge whether the child liked or didn't like the food by looking at his face. Then it's the second child's turn to feed the first. Continue until the plate is empty or a child indicates she is full. You can also ask the child who is tasting the food to close her eyes or wear sunglasses with masking tape over the lenses.

119

Five-Minute Fun

Note: This lesson is a collection of activities to promote learning using the language of your daily routines.

Skills
- categorizing
- listening
- remembering directions
- recognizing attributes
- recognizing object function

Materials
- none

> **Success Tip**
> To keep the game fresh, change the category often.

Procedures

Level 1　　During daily activities, teach the child the concept of categories. When dressing, tell the child he's putting on clothes. Then ask the child to name each piece of clothing as he dresses. Other categories you may want to use include: when taking a bath – body parts; when eating – food; when driving in the car – vehicles; when caring for your pets – animals; when playing – toys; and when brushing teeth – grooming items.

Level 2　　Tell the child the name of a category (animals, colors, food, family members, tools). Ask the child to name at least three items from the category. As the child learns the game, increase the number of items he must name in the category.

Level 3　　Challenge the child by making the categories more specific. For example, you might ask the child, "Tell me an animal that lives in the zoo."

Other suggested categories:

animals:	farm, live in a house, water
food:	fruit, crunchy, candy, breakfast
vehicles:	on the road, in the air, in the water
toys:	build with, ride on, big
clothes:	with buttons, wear in summer, wear in winter
family members:	live far away, boys, have brown hair, grown-ups
furniture:	sit on, living room, made of wood
body parts:	two of, put jewelry on, bend
buildings:	people work in, you go to every day, buy things
tools:	cut with, use outside, fit in a toolbox
beverages:	hot/cold, kids like to drink, sweet

Dialogue Highlights	Talk about what you are doing. Here are some examples.

Level 1
- *Time for a bath. Get in the tub.*
- *You have lots of parts to your body.*
- *I'm washing your hand.*
- *Now what am I washing?*

Level 2
- *I'll name a group. You name three things in that group.*
- *Tell me three animals.*

Level 3
- *Let's play the category game again.*
- *You know lots of buildings.*
- *This time, only tell me buildings where we buy things.*

Extension Activity

Tell the child three items from a general category (dog, cat, horse). Ask the child to name the category (animals). As the child masters this type of categorization, make this activity more challenging by naming more specific categories of objects (duck, frog, fish—animals that live in the water; sheep, cow, pig—farm animals).

Promoting Peer Interaction

Tell the children that it will be important to listen to each other while playing this game. Begin a sentence with "I'm going to the store and I'm going to buy _____." Fill in the blank with something you could buy at a store. Ask the first child to repeat the sentence, repeat your answer, and fill in the blank with his own answer. Have the next child repeat the sentence with your answer, the first child's answer, and his own answer. Continue until all have played the game or for as long as the children are able to remember the sequence of answers. Other sentences you might use:

I'm going to the zoo and I'm going to see _____.
I'm going out to eat and I'll order _____.
I'm looking into outer space and I'll see _____.

I've Got to Be Me

Skills

- recognizing personal information
- recognizing information about family members
- answering questions
- listening
- personal awareness

Materials

- photograph of the child
- photographs of family members
- package of index cards
- markers

Success Tip

When asking the child to compare her written name to another name in print, choose names that start with a different letter and have a different number of letters in them.

In the Promoting Peer Interaction activity, use the same phrases at first until the children are comfortable answering the questions. Then vary the order and wording of the questions, as each situation will be different. If the child relies on exactly worded questions and phrasing, she may be unsuccessful in meeting and greeting new people.

Procedures

Level 1

Talk to the child about her photograph. You might say, "This is a picture of you. You are a girl. You're three years old. You're wearing a blue shirt. Your whole name is Karin Smith." Next show the child photographs of family members, one at a time. Ask the child to name the family members. Then talk about the person's gender, color of clothing, etc. Put the child's photograph with the family members' photographs. Again show the child the photographs one at a time. Ask the child to stand when she sees her photograph. Talk about each person as you show the photograph. Prompt the child to stand if she doesn't recognize her own photo. Repeat the activity until the child recognizes her photograph.

Then show the child two photographs at the same time. Ask her to point to her photograph. Continue the activity until the child can choose her photograph from a pair of photographs.

Levels 2 & 3

Print the child's and five other names on separate index cards. Show the child the card with her name. Draw your finger across the bottom of her name. You might say, "This is your name. It says Karin." Then ask the child to draw her finger across the card while saying her name. Now show all the name cards to the child, one at a time. Ask the child to stand up when she sees her name. Place the child's card on the table with another card. Ask the child to point to her name. Continue practicing.

Present the child with different pairs of cards and randomly alternate placing the child's name on the left and on the right. Each time the child finds her card say, "Yes, what is your name?" Pause to allow her to respond to the question.

Gradually increase the number of cards presented until the child can find her name from the group of six cards. Follow this procedure to teach the following personal information: age (How old are you?), birth date (When's your birthday? [month and date only]), address (Where do you live?), and phone number (What's your phone number?).

Dialogue Highlights

Talk about what you are doing. Here are some examples.

Level 1

- *I'll put the pictures together.*
- *When you see your picture, stand up.*
- *This picture is a boy. He's wearing a red shirt. Good, you knew it was Juan. You didn't stand up.*
- *This picture is a girl. Good. You stood up.*
- *Now here are two pictures. Point to your picture.*

Levels 2 and 3

- *Here's your card. It has your name on it.*
- *What's your name?*
- *Stand up when you see your name.*
- *Here are two names. Which one says "Karin"?*

Extension Activity

Materials: bulletin board

Make an "All About Me" bulletin board. As the child learns the skills in the above activity, put cards on the board that say, "I know my name. My name is _____. I know my address. My address is _____." Be sure to write the date of mastery on the cards. Add notes about other accomplishments like, "I can tie my shoes," or "I can match shapes." Also add the child's artwork, photographs of friends and special activities, greeting cards, and invitations. Each year on the child's birthday, put all the mementos into a scrapbook, and start a new collection.

Promoting Peer Interaction

Practice meeting and greeting new people. Pretend you are going to a friend's house for supper. Teach the children a simple script in which they introduce themselves and answer simple questions about personal information. After you have practiced with each child, have the children work in pairs to role-play meeting and greeting each other.

We're going to my friend Barb's house for supper tonight. Let's practice what you're going to say to Barb. I'll pretend to be Barb.

Barb:	Hi. My name is Barb.
Child:	Hi. My name is John.
Barb:	It's nice to meet you, John. How are you today?
Child:	I'm fine. How are you?
Barb:	I'm fine, too. How old are you?
Child:	I'm 3.
Barb:	Wow! You're 3! You're getting so big.

Your Day of Days

Skills
- making choices
- expressing opinions
- planning future events

Materials
Levels 2 & 3
- large sheet of paper
- markers

Success Tips

For very young children learning to make choices, show the child both choices when possible.

Only offer alternatives that you are willing to let the child select.

Procedures

Level 1   Determine five different times during your daily routine when you can offer your child a choice between two alternatives. Present the alternatives and ask the child to choose what she wants. You might give her a choice of orange juice or milk at breakfast, a choice of red or blue socks, or a choice of watching a TV program or a video. Vary the times as well as the choices offered from day to day. Use words like *choice* and *what you like* as you talk to the child.

Level 2   Tell the child you need her help. You'll need her to make choices early in the day for activities that will happen later in the day. Make a chart with pictures representing the activities. For example, if the child gets to choose her snack food, draw a table. If the child gets to choose her bedtime story, draw a book. Offer the child the two choices for each activity. Record the choices by the picture on the chart. Then when it's time for snack, refer to the chart, and remind the child of her choice.

Level 3   This activity lets the child determine the alternatives and make the selection. Explain that the child gets to plan an activity for the next day. For example, she may get to plan the lunch menu. Ask the child what she likes to eat for lunch. Then tell the child that she can decide what the lunch menu will be. Prompt the child to include the beverage, main dish, and dessert. Write down the selected menu.

When preparing lunch the next day, use the menu to review the child's choices. Other activities to plan include what outfit to wear, a choice of a playmate, a video to rent, and an art activity. If the child suggests an activity that is not an option at that time, explain why it's not possible. For example, if the child wants to visit Grandma and she's six hours away, acknowledge that while that is a fun thing to do, it's not a choice this time.

Dialogue Highlights   Talk about what you are doing. Here are some examples.

Level 1

- *It's time for breakfast.*
- *Do you want juice or milk?*
- *You chose to drink milk.*
- *You like milk.*

Level 2

- *You need to make some choices.*
- *Do you want crackers or pretzels for your snack?*
- *I'll write pretzels on the chart.*
- *That will help us remember that you chose pretzels.*

Level 3

- *What do you like to eat for lunch?*
- *Okay, we'll have macaroni and cheese.*
- *What shall we have to drink?*
- *We can't have root beer floats because we don't have any ice cream.*

Extension Activity   Help the child learn that she can make choices that affect other people. Ask the child to help you select a gift for a familiar person. First talk about what the person likes. Then discuss possible gifts based on what you know about the person's likes. Make a final choice and plan when you will shop. If possible, have the child accompany you when you shop. Other choices that the child could help you plan include which video to rent for her sister to watch, which flavor of ice cream her father would like, or which restaurant her friend would like to go to.

Promoting Peer Interaction   Plan playtime with another child. Ask each child to select one activity for the playtime. Have each child lead the activity she chose. For example, if the child chooses to "read a book," she gets to hold the book and show the pictures to the other child.

Georgie Porgie's Favorite

Skills
- cooking, mixing, pouring
- following directions
- using action words
- exploring adult routines

Materials
- box of instant pudding
- 2 cups of milk
- rotary eggbeater or wire whisk
- mixing bowl
- large spoon
- apron

Success Tips

Be aware of food allergies when cooking with children other than your own.

Before you begin a recipe with a group of children, tell them they'll be able to have a taste at the end of the cooking session.

Procedures

Gather all the ingredients and equipment needed to make the pudding. Have the child wash her hands and put on the apron. Identify the bowl, eggbeater, and spoon for the child.

Level 1   Tell the child that you're going to make pudding. Open the box and ask the child to empty the pudding mix into the bowl. Pour one cup of milk into a measuring cup. Ask the child to pour the milk into the bowl. Repeat this procedure for the second cup of milk. Show the child how the eggbeater works to combine the pudding mix and milk. Then give the child a turn to mix the pudding. Help the child turn the eggbeater if needed. Refrigerate the pudding until ready to eat. Enjoy!

Level 2   Make the pudding following the directions on the box. Read the first step to the child. Have her complete that step. Then read the second step. Complete all steps of the recipe. Help the child as needed.

Level 3   Prepare a mix with more steps, like macaroni and cheese, cookies, or muffins. Ask the child to get the equipment needed for each step. Have the child explain each step of the recipe before proceeding with the direction.

Dialogue Highlights	Talk about what you are doing. Here are some examples.
Level 1	*Let's make pudding!* *Here's a bowl (beater, spoon).* *Pour the pudding into the bowl.* *Do you want to stir?*
Level 2	*I'll read the directions to make pudding.* *Listen. "Pour two cups of milk into the bowl."* *What do we need first?* *I'll help you measure the milk.* *The next direction says, "Add mix." What do you need to do?*
Level 3	*Look! This recipe has five parts.* *First we have to cook the macaroni.* *What will we need to cook the macaroni?* *What do we need to do next?*
Extension Activity	Cook something from a recipe that has few ingredients, like Rice Krispie Treats® made in the microwave. Another easy recipe to make is:

Peanut Butter Cookies

Combine one egg, one cup of sugar, and one cup of peanut butter. Drop by spoonfuls onto a cookie sheet. Bake at 350 degrees for 8 to 10 minutes. Watch carefully, as these cookies burn easily.

Promoting Peer Interaction	Materials: jar, instant pudding mix
	Ask several children to help make pudding in a jar. Use an instant pudding mix. Combine all ingredients in a wide-mouth jar. Screw the lid on tightly. Have each child shake the jar 10 times before passing the jar to the next child. Continue shaking until the pudding has thickened. Serve.

Wrap It Up!

Skills
- taping, folding, and tying
- following directions
- using the words *long*, *short*, *first*, *next,* and *last*
- improving hand-eye coordination

Materials
- gift box
- enough gift wrap to wrap the box
- scissors
- ribbon and bow
- heavy tape dispenser

Levels 2 & 3
- additional gift wrap
- small toy

Success Tips

Use wrapping paper that is packaged in a flat square. Have the child use the fold lines of the paper as a guide when cutting.

Practice this activity before an event, like a friend's birthday, that will require a wrapped package.

Procedures

Place the tape dispenser in a box and wrap it like a present.

Level 1   Show the wrapped package to the child. Talk about the bow, the tape, and the wrapping paper. Ask the child to guess what's inside the package. Have the child tear off the paper to open the package. Take the tape dispenser out of the box and name it.

Show the child how the tape dispenser works. Then allow the child to tear off a length of tape. Assist the child if needed. When the child understands how to use the tape dispenser, tear off a short length of tape. Describe the tape as *short*. Attach one end of the tape to the edge of the table. Ask the child to tear off a short piece. Next tear off a longer length of tape. Describe the tape as *long*. Attach one end of the tape to the edge of the table. Tell the child to tear off a long piece. Compare the two lengths of tape. Have the child continue to tear off short and long lengths of tape and put them on the edge of the table by other pieces of tape that are the same length.

Level 2   Place a small toy in a box and wrap it like a present. Show the wrapped package to the child. Talk about the bow, the tape, and the wrapping paper. Ask the child to guess what's inside the package. Have the child tear off the paper to open the package.

Tell the child that you need her help to rewrap the package. Have the child put the toy back in the box. Assist the child in measuring a length of paper, cutting the paper, wrapping the paper around the box, and taping the paper. Add a bow. Describe the action at each step.

Note: In most cases, the child will not want to keep the toy, as she is more interested in the tape, paper, and wrapping process.

Level 3 Introduce the child to wrapping and unwrapping presents with the Level 2 activity. Then ask the child to find a small item he wants to wrap. Have the child arrange the materials needed to wrap the package in the order they will be used. Use words like *first, next,* and *last.* Ask the child to wrap the package. Help him as needed.

Dialogue Highlights Talk about what you are doing. Here are some examples.

Level 1
- *Look! I have a present. What's in it?*
- *Let's open the present.*
- *Watch me tear off tape.*
- *Lift the tape. Pull the tape. Pull down. Tear off the tape.*
- *I tear off a short piece.*
- *You tear off a short piece.*

Level 2
- *I have a present wrapped in paper.*
- *See the paper and the bow?*
- *What's in the package?*
- *Now you get to wrap a package.*
- *Put the car in the box.*
- *We need the wrapping paper.*

Level 3
- *Can you find something to put in our box?*
- *Now let's wrap the box.*
- *What do we do first?*
- *What do we use next?*

Extension Activity Materials: scraps of wrapping paper, bows, tape, a sheet of construction paper

Use scraps of wrapping paper and bows to make a collage. Show the child how to tear off small pieces of wrapping paper. Then have her tape the pieces of paper to a sheet of construction paper to make a collage.

Promoting Peer Interaction

Have two children work together to wrap a package. Promote interaction through the following steps.

1. Have one child put the toy in the box and the other child put the lid on the box.
2. Have one child measure the paper and the other child cut the paper.
3. Have one child wrap the paper around the box and hold it in place.
4. Have the other child tape the paper closed.
5. Have one child fold one end of the paper and the other child tape the end closed.
6. Have the children switch jobs to close the other end of the package.
7. Have one child measure ribbon and the other child cut ribbon.
8. Have one child tape the ribbon in place and the other child add a bow.

Flip Your Lid

Skills

- matching a lid to a container
- making decisions
- using the words *on*, *off*, *turn*, *twist*, *open*, *closed*, *try*, and *hold*
- screwing and unscrewing lids

Materials

- an assortment of containers with screw-top lids like plastic spice jars, shampoo or detergent bottles, and jars
- markers or colored tape

Level 2
- extra non-matching lids

Level 3
- puzzle or pegboard and pegs

Success Tip

Keep an assortment of containers and lids available near your work area. Store them on a low shelf or in a bottom cupboard to allow the child access to them while you work.

Procedures

Use markers or colored tape to color-code the containers and their lids.

Level 1   Show the child a container with its lid on and a container with its lid off. Say the words *on* and *off*. Encourage the child to repeat the words. Ask the child if the lid fits. Show the child how to twist the lid on and off.

Give the child a container with its lid on. Give the child time to practice twisting the lid on and off. Use words like *turn*, *twist*, *open*, and *closed* to talk about what the child is doing. Then hold up a container and a lid that obviously don't fit together. Try to put the lid on the container as you talk about what you're doing.

Level 2   Show the child a container with its lid on and a container with its lid off. Use the words *on*, *off*, *open*, and *closed* to talk about the containers. Then give the child a container, its lid, and a lid that doesn't fit the container. Encourage the child to choose the lid that fits and to put it on the container. Use words like *try*, *turn*, *twist*, and *hold* to talk about what the child is doing. When the child has found the correct lid, have her exchange containers and lids and try again.

Level 3   Put a puzzle piece or a peg into each container and screw on the lid. Show the child a container with its lid on and a container with its lid off. Ask the child to tell which container is open, which container is closed, which lid is on, and which lid is off. Then give the child three containers with puzzle pieces or pegs inside them. Encourage the child to open the containers and remove the pieces or pegs. Have the child leave the lids off the containers as she plays with the puzzle or pegboard. When the child is finished with the puzzle or pegboard, challenge her to put the lids back onto the correct containers. Use words like *turn, twist, hold,* and *try* to talk about what the child is doing. Promote daily practice of this skill by asking the child to open and close containers during routine activities like cooking or bathing.

Dialogue Highlights

Talk about what you are doing. Here are some examples.

Level 1

- *Look. I have two jars.*
- *This jar has a lid.*
- *The lid is on.*
- *Does this lid fit this jar?*
- *Let's twist the lid off.*
- *Now let's put the lid back on. Turn it.*

Level 2

- *Is the lid on or off this jar?*
- *This jar is open.*
- *Here is a jar for you and here are two lids.*
- *Try both lids.*
- *Hold the jar.*
- *Twist the lid.*

Level 3

- *Look at these containers. We use them to put things in.*
- *Which container is open?*
- *There's something inside these containers.*
- *Open them to see what's inside.*
- *Twist the lids.*
- *Let's put the puzzle together.*
- *Now let's put the lids back on the containers.*
- *Which lid fits this container?*

Extension Activity

Give the child an uncovered container. Put the matching lid and three lids that are of similar size but not interchangeable next to the container. Put the matching lid third in the line of four lids. Tell the child to find the right lid for the container. Ask the child to try the first lid. Let the child try the lid on the container. Ask the child if the lid fits. When the child says, "No," coach her to move that lid away from the other lids. Then have her try the next lid in line. Repeat the procedure. Then have the child try the third lid. Ask the child if the lid fits. When the child says, "Yes," point to the remaining lid. Ask the child if she needs to try the last lid. Explain that it's not necessary to try the last lid because she already found the lid that fits. Repeat this activity and vary the position of the matching lid in the line.

Promoting Peer Interaction

Give each child three uncovered containers. Put the matching lids in a bag along with a lid that does not match any of the containers in the bag. Ask the children to match the lids in the bag to their containers. Have the first child select a lid and try to match the lid to one of her containers. If the lid doesn't match any of the child's containers, ask her to decide which of the other children's containers looks like it matches. Prompt the child to offer the lid to the child with the matching container or have that child request the container from the first child. Continue the game until all containers and lids have been matched.

Dish It Up

Skills
- naming foods
- making decisions
- learning the concepts *healthy* and *unhealthy*
- following directions
- cutting with scissors

Materials
- paper plates
- several food and non-food items

Level 2
- several pictures of food and non-food items cut from magazines

Level 3
- several pictures of healthy and unhealthy food items cut from magazines
- magazine with several pictures of healthy and unhealthy foods
- piece of poster board or sturdy paper
- tape
- scissors
- grocery bag

Success Tips

Help the child tear the page from the magazine before cutting out the picture.

Outline magazine pictures with a wide-tipped marker. This provides the child with a line to follow while cutting.

Procedures

Level 1   Give the child a paper plate. Show the child a food item. Ask the child if the item can be eaten. Then present a non-food item. Again ask the child if the item can be eaten. Then ask the child to put the food item on her plate.

Next present one food and one non-food item at the same time. Ask the child to put the food item on her plate. Continue until the child has selected all the food items and put them on her plate.

Level 2   Place the magazine pictures on the table. Give the child a paper plate. Tell the child to pretend she's in a cafeteria. Have her walk along the table. Ask her to choose three pictures of things she can eat. Then have the child sit down. Ask her to hold up her pictures and name them. Talk about the child's choices. Encourage the child to tell why she didn't choose the pictures left on the table.

Level 3   Show the child the pictures of foods. Talk about why some foods are healthy to eat and why other foods aren't healthy to eat. Tape several pictures of healthy foods onto a sturdy piece of paper or poster board to remind the child about healthy foods.

Then give the child a magazine and scissors. Have her cut out pictures of healthy foods from the magazine. Mix these pictures with pictures of unhealthy foods and put them on the table.

Tell the child to pretend she has a new job. She'll shop for groceries for a restaurant. She can only buy healthy foods. Give the child a grocery bag. Ask her to put the pictures of healthy food into the grocery bag. Encourage the child to talk about what's in her grocery bag.

Dialogue Highlights

Talk about what you are doing. Here are some examples.

Level 1
- *Here's your plate.*
- *Let's talk about what we can eat.*
- *Can we eat an apple?*
- *Can we eat a book?*
- *Choose the one we eat.*
- *Put the raisins on your plate.*

Level 2
- *Let's pretend we're in a cafeteria.*
- *In a cafeteria, you pick out the food you want to eat.*
- *Pick up three pictures of food.*
- *What did you choose to eat?*
- *Here's a picture of a car. Why didn't you take this picture?*

Level 3
- *I have pictures of food.*
- *What is this?*
- *Apples are healthy foods.*
- *Candy bars taste good, but they can be bad for your teeth.*
- *Let's tape pictures of healthy foods on this paper.*
- *Now it's your turn to find pictures of healthy foods.*
- *Let's pretend you are shopping for a restaurant. You can only buy healthy foods.*
- *When you're done shopping, you can show me what you bought.*

Extension Activity

A trip to the grocery store can help the child practice finding healthy and unhealthy foods.

Dish It Up, *continued*

Promoting Peer Interaction

Materials: containers of healthy and unhealthy foods, grocery bags, trays or cookie sheets

Play a *Healthy Foods* relay game. Put a table at one end of the room and place containers of healthy and unhealthy foods on it. Have each team of children stand at the other end of the room. Put a grocery bag by each team. Give the first two children on each team a tray or cookie sheet. Have each child hold one end of the tray and practice walking together.

To start the game, have the first two members of each team carry their tray to the table. Tell each team to pick out a healthy food item and put it on their tray. Have the team carry the tray back to start and put the food into the bag. Continue until the team has selected all the healthy food items. To add to the fun, set a timer. Challenge the children to get all the healthy foods into the grocery bag before the timer rings.

Strategies for Learning Through Games

> "When children are playing games, their interest and motivation work together to create a wonderful learning opportunity."[1]

Games can provide a fun, relaxed atmosphere to teach new skills or to practice skills already learned. Playing board games is a recreational activity that can be enjoyed by all ages. In addition to learning specific concepts such as shapes or colors, games can also be used to teach social skills like following directions and rules, taking turns, cooperation, and good sportsmanship. In this section, you will find a variety of games for skill practice as well as a series of activities to teach board game skills.

Set the stage for a successful learning experience by:

- providing a comfortable work area. It may be easier to work at a table than to sit on the floor when manipulating a variety of objects or pieces.

- removing distractions from the work area. Some children work better in a quiet spot without posters or pictures on the walls. If the game has lots of pieces, you may want to keep some out of sight in a tub or bag until needed.

- allowing the child to hold and manipulate the materials to be used in the game before beginning to play. Name the items for the child. Then collect the materials before starting the game.

- demonstrating the activity for the child and allowing the child to practice before playing the game.

- teaching the game to the child individually before expecting the child to play with a group.

- modifying the activity as needed.

- teaching good sportsmanship. Model appropriate comments for the child like, "I had fun playing with you," "Wow, you matched all the pictures," or "Great, you made it to the end!"

When playing with puzzles:

- use a tray or mat to define the work area and keep the pieces close at hand.

- hand pieces to the child one at a time or give the child a choice of two pieces.

- use verbal prompts or hand-over-hand to help the child make a piece fit.

[1]Feldman, 1994.

- take turns with the child, each of you putting in one piece at a time.

- begin with puzzles with just a few pieces that don't interlock and work toward puzzles with many interlocking pieces.

- select puzzles with larger pieces or knobbed pieces for beginners.

- provide a variety of puzzles for the child to put together, insuring that she learns the skill of putting puzzles together rather than just putting a particular puzzle together.

- put all the pieces of the puzzle into a bag and let the child select one at a time for added fun. For more of a challenge, put the pieces from two puzzles into a bag. The child can discard pieces not in his puzzle or he can put both puzzles together at the same time. (Note: Mark the backs of the puzzle pieces for ease in sorting.)

When playing games:

- practice the skills required before beginning the game, such as rolling the dice, moving a token, or selecting a card.

- use simple game boards with fewer spaces at first. Try to select a game board without a lot of illustrations that may distract the child. To shorten the game, cover part of the game path with paper, changing the starting or stopping point. You can also play the game for a set number of turns or a set length of time.

- use fewer cards or pieces when teaching the game. For example, when playing CandyLand®, use only the cards with one colored square at first. Then add the picture cards or double square cards. Lastly, follow the directions for the spaces with black dots on the game board.

- introduce games like Tic-Tac-Toe that require the child to make choices or use strategies after the child has mastered basic skills like rolling the dice.

- encourage the child to help modify the game by thinking up new rules for a favorite game.

- present a variety of games to keep the child's interest high and to insure generalization of game-playing skills. (Note: Yard or garage sales may be good sources for board games. Even if parts are missing, you can use the game boards, dice, spinners, or tokens to create your own games.)

- don't always play to win. Sometimes play until all have completed the activity. Demonstrate how to win and how to lose graciously.

Developmental Sequence for Games

- o puts together 3 – 4 piece shape puzzle

- o puts together 3 – 4 piece puzzle with non-interlocking pieces

- o puts together 4-piece nesting toy

- o stacks 3 – 5 blocks

- o matches lotto cards to board

- o stacks 7 – 9 blocks

- o matches colored blocks

- o puts together two parts of a picture to make a whole picture

- o puts together 6 – 10 piece puzzle with non-interlocking pieces

- o puts together 3 – 5 piece puzzle with interlocking pieces

- o puts together 6 – 10 piece puzzle with interlocking pieces

140   *For Parents & Professionals: Preschool*

Tic-Tac-Match

Skills
- matching objects to pictures or outlines
- naming objects

Materials
- marker
- scissors
- ruler
- large bag
- 12" x 12" piece of cardboard
- one set of 9 small objects like a comb, a doll shoe, a block, a toy car
- picture of each of the 9 objects

Level 3
- outline drawings of the 9 objects (You might need to place the objects on light-colored paper and trace around them with a dark marker.)

Success Tips
Take photographs of the objects. Order double prints to use for two game boards or a picture-to-picture matching activity.

The prizes given to children in fast-food restaurants can be interesting objects to include in this game.

Procedures

Make a Tic-Tac-Match picture board. Use a marker to divide the piece of cardboard into nine 4" squares.

Level 1 Put a pictured object in each square of the Tic-Tac-Match board and give it to the child. Name each picture. Next show the child the matching set of objects. Name each object. Have the child point to the picture of the object on the picture board.

Then put the objects into the bag. Have the child choose an object from the bag. Name the object and have the child find the matching picture on the picture board. Ask the child to put the object on the matching picture. Continue the activity until the child has covered the board with objects.

Level 2 Put a pictured object in each square on the Tic-Tac-Match board and give it to the child. Ask the child to name each picture. Demonstrate making "three in a row" going up, down, across, and diagonally on the board using the matching objects. Practice until the child understands the concept of "three in a row." Then put the objects into the bag. Have the child choose an object and put the object on the matching picture. Play until the child "wins" by matching three objects in a row.

Level 3   Put the outline drawings of the objects in each square on the Tic-Tac-Match picture board and give it to the child. Ask the child to point to each outline as you name it. Then show the objects to the child. As you name each object, have the child point to the outline on her picture board. Talk about the details of each outline that will help the child make a match. You might say, "Look at the circles at the bottom of this outline. They look like tires. This outline looks like a car." Demonstrate making "three in a row" on the board using the matching objects. Practice until the child understands the concept of "three in a row."

Put the set of objects into the bag. Have the child choose an object from the bag, name it, and match it to an outline on the picture board. Play until the child "wins" by matching three objects in a row.

Dialogue   Talk about what you are doing. Here are some examples.
Highlights

Level 1   • *Look at your picture board.*
           • *Find the picture of each thing I show you.*
           • *Here's a block.*
           • *Find the block on your picture board.*

Level 2   • *Look! You matched all the pictures.*
           • *The blocks, the shoe, and the comb are in a row.*
           • *Three in a row.*
           • *One, two, three in a row up and down.*
           • *Now you show me three in a row.*

Level 3   • *These pictures are called outlines. An outline shows the shape of an object.*
           • *Listen while I name each outline. Then point to the outline on your picture board.*
           • *Now I'll show you some things. Here's a car.*
           • *Find the outline of a car on your board.*
           • *Put the car on your picture board.*
           • *Do you have three in a row?*
           • *Now you choose a toy from the bag.*
           • *Can you find the outline on your picture board?*

142   Games
For Parents & Professionals: Preschool

Extension Activities

Materials: large bag, Tic-Tac-Match boards, objects that match and don't match the pictures on the picture boards

When you fill the game bag, include objects that don't match any of the pictures on the picture boards. Then play Tic-Tac-Match.

For a greater challenge, play Tic-Tac-Match by matching pictures to the outlines. Make additional game boards for specific categories like animals, foods, or toys.

Promoting Peer Interaction

Materials: 18 small objects, pictures of the 18 objects, Tic-Tac-Match boards

Note: You may want to look through magazines for pictures of common objects and then gather the objects based on the pictures.

Collect 18 small objects and divide them into two sets. Make corresponding picture boards for each set of objects. Put all of the objects into one bag. Give each child a game board. Have one child pick an object out of the bag. Then have him look to see if the object is pictured on his game board. If the child doesn't have a match, have him offer the object to the other child. Have the children alternate turns.

Getting the Whole Picture

Skills

- identifying a whole from its parts
- naming attributes
- naming pictured objects
- answering *wh*-questions

Materials

- several large pictures of objects cut from magazines

Levels 2 & 3

- four 8 1/2" x 11" sheets of cardboard
- scissors
- several large pictures of objects from categories like animals and toys

Success Tips

Select magazine pictures that have common, familiar objects. Parenting magazines are good sources for pictures of common objects.

Use photographs of family members and pictures of family outings. The child may particularly enjoy photographs of himself as a baby.

After you cut apart the pictures, make a mark on the wrong side of each piece so you can correctly position the pieces when putting them together.

Procedures

Level 1

Cut a magazine picture in half horizontally, vertically, or diagonally. Show the child how to put the two halves of the picture together to make a whole. Identify what the picture is. Tell the child he'll match halves of pictures to make whole pictures.

Choose a new picture. Put half of the picture on the table. Then put the other half of the picture and half of a different picture on the table. Ask the child to choose the half that fits with the half on the table to make a whole picture. Point out clues in the pictures that show which halves fit together. Continue mixing and matching pictures until the child can easily put them together.

Level 2

Cut a 1" square out of the center of a sheet of cardboard, a 2" square out of the center of a second sheet of cardboard, a 4" square out of a third sheet, and a 6" square out of a fourth sheet. You'll use the cardboard sheets to cover pictures during the activity.

Show the child two complete pictures. Encourage the child to name each picture. Then put one of the pictures facedown on the table. Cover the other picture with the sheet of cardboard with the 1" cutout. Ask the child to look in the cutout area and guess what the picture is. Each time the child guesses what the picture is, ask him to tell which part of the picture he saw.

If the child can't guess what the picture is, use the cover with the 2" cutout so the child can see more of the picture. Continue to change covers, letting the child see more of the covered picture. Repeat this activity until the child can identify all of the pictures.

Level 3   Prepare sheets of cardboard as described in Level 2. Choose a picture without showing it to the child. Put the cover sheet with the 1" cutout over the picture. Tell the child which category the picture belongs in (animals, toys). Ask the child to tell what part he sees through the cutout. Then have him guess what the picture is.

If the child can't guess what the picture is, use the cover with the 2" cutout so the child can see more of the picture. Continue to change covers, letting the child see more of the covered picture. Repeat this activity until the child can identify all of the pictures.

Dialogue Highlights   Talk about what you are doing. Here are some examples.

Level 1
- *This picture shows the top of an apple. This picture shows the bottom of an apple. They go together to make a whole apple.*
- *Now you put the picture together.*
- *The green spot on the top matches the green spot down here.*
- *It's a leaf.*

Level 2
- *Here is a picture of a deer. Here is a picture of a rabbit. I'll cover one of the pictures with this card.*
- *You can see some of the picture through this hole.*
- *Can you guess which animal is hiding behind the card?*
- *What part of the animal do you see?*

Level 3
- *Look through the hole.*
- *What do you think you see?*
- *We haven't guessed what this picture is yet.*
- *Let's use a cover with a bigger hole in it.*
- *Now what do you see?*

Extension Activities   Materials: cutout cardboard covers, pictures of common animals/objects

Give a point value to each card cover used. For example, the cover with the smallest hole can have the highest point value. The child gets the point value of the cover card used when he names the picture.

Materials: toys

Put several toys in front of the child. Name parts of one toy without telling the name of the toy. Ask the child to guess which toy you are describing.

Promoting Peer Interaction

Cut the magazine pictures into four to six pieces. Mix up the puzzle pieces and place them facedown on a surface. Have the first child turn over one picture piece and show it to the second child. Ask the children if they can identify the whole picture. If they can't guess what the picture is, have the second child turn over a piece. Continue until the children assemble and identify the picture.

146

Games
For Parents & Professionals: Preschool

Color Match

Skills
- matching colors
- naming colors

Materials
- 1 large sheet of red paper
- 1 large sheet of yellow paper
- 12 red toys
- 12 yellow toys
- a large bag

Level 3
- several pictures of red objects
- several pictures of yellow objects

Success Tip
Select toys with the same shade of each color as you introduce this activity.

Procedures

Level 1   Put the red and yellow sheets of paper in front of the child. Name the colors of the paper. Show the child the bag of toys. Choose a toy from the bag and name the color. Explain to the child the toy belongs on the paper that's the same color.

Then have the child choose a toy from the bag. Name the toy and tell what color it is. Encourage the child to put the toy on the paper of the same color. Continue until all the toys are on the correct sheets of paper.

After black and white, red and yellow are considered to be the easiest colors to discriminate between.

Level 2   Show the child the red and yellow paper and the bag of toys. Have the child choose a toy from the bag. Ask the child to name the toy and its color and then put the toy on the sheet of paper that's the same color. Continue the activity until each toy is on the correct sheet of paper. Then ask the child to find something in the room that is either yellow or red. Talk about the object the child finds.

Level 3   Show the child the red and yellow paper and the bag of toys. Have the child choose a toy, name it, and put it on the sheet of paper that's the same color. Continue until all toys are on the right sheets of paper. Next put the pictures of red and yellow objects into the bag. Have the child choose a picture from the bag and name it. Talk about which color the picture matches. Have the child put the picture on the right sheet of paper.

Color Match, *continued*

Dialogue Highlights Talk about what you are doing. Here are some examples.

Level 1
- *Look at these sheets of paper. This paper is red. This paper is yellow.*
- *I have toys in this bag.*
- *Some of the toys are red. They go on the red paper.*
- *Choose a toy from the bag.*
- *You found a red ball. Where does the red ball belong?*
- *Good. Put the red ball on the red paper.*

Level 2
- *Choose a toy from the bag.*
- *What toy did you find?*
- *What color is the car?*
- *Put the yellow car on the yellow paper.*
- *Nice matching.*
- *Now look around the room. Can you find something yellow?*
- *Which paper does the book match?*

Level 3
- *What did you find in the bag?*
- *Which paper does the red truck go on?*
- *Which picture did you choose?*
- *Put the red coat on the red paper.*

Extension Activities Introduce a third color into any level of the activity as the child becomes successful working with two colors.

Practice matching colors by sorting buttons, crayons, or blocks.

Have the child help match socks by their colors while doing laundry.

Promoting Peer Interaction Play a version of the children's game *I Spy* based on color. Ask one child to cover his eyes. Tell the second child to touch a red object somewhere in the room and return to you. Then have the first child uncover his eyes and guess the name of the object by saying, "I spy something red. Is it the red pillow?" If the guess is incorrect, the second child gives a clue. Have the first child continue guessing until he identifies the object. To simplify this game, place five objects of the same color in front of the children. Continue with the game as described above.

What's Under There?

Skills
- identifying and naming objects
- answering and asking *yes/no* and *wh*-questions
- recognizing something is missing

Materials
- variety of common objects
- hat

Success Tips

To increase the number of *yes/no* questions a child will answer, guess the name of the hidden object last.

When playing the phone game in the Extension Activity, make it clear to the child that there is a difference between the phone game and other telephone calls. This will help maintain appropriate phone behavior.

Procedures

Place three objects on a table. Ask the child to name the objects. Give the child a hat. Tell the child to cover one of the objects with the hat while you close your eyes. (You might want to peek a little!) Have the child put the two uncovered objects on his lap out of sight.

Level 1   Guess which object is under the hat by asking, "Is it the sock?" Continue asking *yes/no* questions until you have guessed the object. Continue having the child hide objects under the hat.

Level 2   Guess which object is under the hat by asking, "Is it the sock?" Continue asking questions until you have guessed the object. Then take a turn hiding the object while the child guesses what is hidden. If the child says "Key?" as his guess, model a more complete question by saying, "Is it the key?" Then pause to provide an opportunity for the child to imitate you. If the child does not imitate you, model the question form again and continue with the game.

Level 3   Guess which object is under the hat by asking, "Is it the sock?" If you do not correctly guess using a *yes/no* question, ask the question "What do you do with it?" before asking a second *yes/no* question. Continue asking questions until you have guessed the object. Then take a turn hiding the object while the child guesses what is hidden. If the child's guess using a *yes/no* question is not correct, prompt the child to ask a *wh*-question ("What do you do with it?"). Pause so the child can imitate you. If the child does not imitate you, model the question form again and answer the question. Have the child continue to ask questions until he guesses the object.

Dialogue Highlights
Talk about what you are doing. Here are some examples.

Level 1
- *Tell me what you see on the table.*
- *You see a sock, a key, and a cup.*
- *I'll close my eyes.*
- *Put the hat on one of the things. Put the other things in your lap.*
- *I'll guess what you hid.*
- *Is it the key?*

Level 2
- *Now it's my turn.*
- *Cover your eyes and I'll hide something under the hat.*
- *Open your eyes and ask me what I hid.*
- *Is it the sock?*

Level 3
- *No, it's not the sock.*
- *What else can you ask me?*
- *Yes, what do you do with it? That's a good question.*
- *You drink from it.*
- *Yes, it's the cup!*

Extension Activities
Materials: magazine pictures of familiar objects

Arrange to have a family member or other adult call the child. Answer the call. Then ask the child to guess who the caller is using *yes/no* questions like, "Is it Aunt Marilyn?" If the guess is incorrect, give the child a clue about the caller's identity and ask him to guess again. Continue giving clues until the child guesses correctly. Then let the child talk to the caller.

Using pictures of familiar objects from a magazine, cut out one feature from each picture. Show a picture to the child and ask, "What's missing?" If the child is unable to identify the missing part, provide a clue or show the child two or three pieces that have been cut out of different pictures. When the child has identified the missing part, have him put the right piece in the picture.

Promoting Peer Interaction

Materials: large umbrella

Open the umbrella and place it on the floor. Have several children sit in a circle. Ask each child to say his name and have the other children repeat it. Then select a child to hide under the umbrella. Ask another child, "Who is under the umbrella?" When the child answers, pretend to knock on the umbrella. Ask the hidden child, "Are you (name given by the child guessing)?" If the hidden child answers, "Yes," lift the umbrella. If the hidden child answers, "No," give the child guessing another chance to name the hidden child. You can help the child who is guessing by giving clues like, "It's a boy. He is wearing a striped shirt." If the child guessing can't name the hidden child, give him two names from which to choose or ask another child to help.

For a more challenging game, ask one child to leave the room or cover his eyes. Ask a second child to hide under the umbrella. When the second child is completely hidden, ask the child guessing to come into the room or open his eyes. Continue as before to guess who is hiding.

Games People Play 1

Skills
- taking turns
- drawing a card
- matching colors
- moving a game token forward
- understanding the concepts *start/end*
- using game vocabulary
- following directions
- understanding one-to-one correspondence

Materials
- game board and game cards (pages 168 – 170)
- red, blue, yellow, green, orange, and purple crayons or markers
- tape
- scissors

Level 2
- game tokens like buttons or pennies

Level 3
- game tokens like erasers or tiny plastic figures

Success Tips

Shorten game-playing periods by reducing the number of game cards in the stack or by going through the stack of cards only once.

Place game markers in a container at the top of the game board rather than in front of the child.

Procedures

Reproduce the game board on pages 168 and 169. Tape the pages together to connect the trains. Randomly color the squares on the game board red, blue, yellow, green, orange, and purple.

Make two copies of the game cards on page 170. Color three each red, blue, yellow, green, orange, and purple. Cut them apart.

Level 1   Show the child the game board. Point to one train and tell the child the squares are different colors. Name each color and ask the child to repeat the color names. Then show the child the color cards. Ask the child to name the colors or name them yourself. Stack the cards color-side down in a pile. Demonstrate how to choose the top card from the stack. Point out the color on the card. Point to a square of the same color on one train on the game board. Discard the game card next to the stack, color-side up. Ask the child to take a turn. Continue until all game cards have been used.

Level 2   Have the child choose a train engine on the game board. Help the child trace his finger along one train. Tell the child that this is the train he will use to play the game. Trace your finger along the other train. Tell the child that this is the train you will use to play the game.

Explain to the child that he will have to take turns while you play the game and that everyone can't play at the same time. Remind the child to keep his hands in his lap so he won't touch things when it's not his turn. Show the child the color cards. Ask the child to name the colors or name them yourself. Stack the cards color-side down in a pile. Demonstrate how to choose the top card from the stack. Point out the color on the card. Ask the child to find a square of the same color on his train. Have him put a marker on that square. Discard the game card next to the stack, color-side up. If no squares of the game card color are open on the game board, the player has to pass his turn. Alternate turns with the child until all game cards have been used.

Level 3

Help the child choose a train as described in Level 2. Give the child a game token and have the child put the token on his train engine. Point to the word "Start" on the game board. Explain to the child that this is where you start playing the game. Point to the word "End" on the game board. Explain that the first person to reach this square wins the game.

Have the child choose a color card. Help the child move his token to the first square of that color on his train. With each turn, move to the next square indicated on the game card. Take turns moving down the path until one person reaches the end of the train track.

Dialogue Highlights

Talk about what you are doing. Here are some examples.

Level 1

- *Let's learn to play a game.*
- *This is the board. We need it to play the game.*
- *Look at the pretty colors.*
- *Here are the cards.*
- *Pick up a card. Turn it over. What color do you see?*
- *Show me a red box on the board.*
- *Now put the card down here. Pick another card.*

Level 2

- *Let's play a game together.*
- *We need rules to play games.*
- *The first rule is to take turns.*
- *First you take a turn on this train. Then put your hands down while I take a turn on this train.*
- *We put markers on the squares.*
- *Choose a card. It's red.*
- *Let's find a red square on your path.*
- *Put your marker on the red square.*

Level 3

- *Here are game tokens.*
- *We use the tokens on the path. Take a token and put it on your train.*
- *This word says "Start."*
- *This word says "End."*
- *Pick a card.*
- *Where is the first orange square?*
- *Move your token to that square.*
- *Now it's my turn.*

Extension Activity

Materials: commercially available board game like CandyLand®

Introduce the child to a commercial board game like CandyLand®. Select a game token and give the child a game token. Put your token at the start of the game. Ask the child to do the same. Trace your finger over the game path until you reach the end. Explain to the child that the first person to reach the end of the path wins the game. Have the child choose a color card. Alternate taking turns. Return discarded game cards to the stack as needed. Continue until the first person reaches the end.

(Note: Modify the game by using only single square color cards. On the board, ignore the black dots which require the player to stay on that square until a specific color card is drawn.)

Promoting Peer Interaction

Board games are interactive by nature. Invite a friend/classmate of the child's to play. Guide them through the rules of a new board game.

Games People Play 2

Skills

- taking turns
- rolling a die
- moving tokens on a game board
- using game vocabulary
- following directions
- one-to-one correspondence

Materials

- die
- game board (pages 168 – 169)
- red, blue, yellow, green, orange, and purple crayons or markers
- scissors

Levels 2 & 3

- game tokens like erasers or tiny plastic figures

Success Tips

Have the child roll the die in a box lid so the die doesn't fall on the floor.

To shorten the game-playing periods, cover a portion of the game board with paper and create a new ending point.

Procedures

Level 1
Show the child the die. Point to the dots. Count the dots with the child. Show the child how to roll the die. Have the child hold the die in his hand, turn his hand over, and drop the die on the table. Ask the child to count the dots on the top of the die. Explain to the child that the number of dots on top of the die is his number. Ask the child to give you the die for your turn. Continue taking turns rolling the die and counting the dots until the child understands the concept.

Level 2
Prepare the game board and familiarize the child with the game board and tokens as described in *Games People Play 1* (pages 152 – 154). Have the child roll the die. Ask him to count the number of dots. Help him move his token the correct number of spaces on his train as you count aloud. Encourage the child to count with you. Then ask the child to give the die to you. Take turns until the first person reaches the end of his train. You don't need to roll the exact number to land on the end square.

Level 3
Use a single train path and have both tokens move along the same path. Help the child through the steps of the game until both players reach the end of the path. If two tokens land on the same space in this game, the tokens can share the space.

Then explain to the child that you're going to play a new game. This time, if two players land on the same space, the first player must go back to start. Move tokens on the game board to demonstrate "going back to start" before playing the game. Take turns until a player reaches the end square.

Dialogue Highlights   Talk about what you are doing. Here are some examples.

Level 1
- *Let's learn more about playing games.*
- *This is called a die. Look at the dots. You roll the die and count the dots.*
- *Hold the die in your hand. Turn your hand over. Now drop the die.*
- *Let's count the dots. One-two-three.*
- *Give me the die, please. It's my turn.*

Level 2
- *It's your turn to roll the die.*
- *What's your number? Three? You move three squares.*
- *Now it's my turn.*
- *Thank you for giving me the die.*

Level 3
- *This time we'll both use your track. I'll put my token by yours.*
- *You can go first.*
- *You rolled three. Move your token three squares.*
(Second game)
- *It's my turn.*
- *I got four. I move my token four squares.*
- *On no, my token lands where your token is! You have to go back to "Start."*

Extension Activity   Materials: commercially available board game like Chutes and Ladders®

Introduce the child to a commercial board game.

Promoting Peer Interaction   Board games are interactive by nature. Invite a friend/classmate of the child's to play. Guide them through the rules of a different board game than in *Games People Play 1*.

Games People Play 3

Skills
- taking turns
- following directions from a game card
- taking more than one turn
- losing a turn
- moving a game token (forward, forward more than one space, backward)
- using game vocabulary

Materials
- game board (pages 168 – 169)
- game tokens
- "Stop" and "Go" cards (pages 171 – 173)

Level 2
- "Go Back" cards (page 173)

Level 3
- "Take 2 Turns," "Move 3," and "Move 4" cards (pages 174 – 175)

Success Tip

People associate the color *red* with "stop" and the color *green* with "go." Color the "Stop" and "Go" game cards red or green to help the child remember whether to stop or go.

Procedures

Prepare the game board as in *Games People Play 1*. Familiarize the child with the game board and tokens as described in *Games People Play 1*. Duplicate and cut apart the "Stop" and "Go" cards on pages 171 – 173.

Level 1   Use one game track per player. Show the child the different game cards. Explain to the child that when he draws a "Stop" card, he must stop and lose his turn. He must not move his token. When he draws a "Go" card, he will move his token forward one square.

Place the "Stop" and "Go" cards in a pile. Ask the child to draw the top card from the deck. Help him decide whether he drew a "Stop" card or a "Go" card. Talk about whether he will move his token or lose his turn. Continue taking turns drawing cards and moving tokens until one player reaches the end.

Level 2   Show the child a "Go Back" card. Explain that he must go back one space on the board if he gets this card. Then shuffle all of the "Go Back" cards into the stack. Help the child when he draws a "Go Back" card until he understands the concept. Continue taking turns drawing cards and moving tokens until one player reaches the end.

Level 3   Show the child a "Take 2 Turns" card. Explain this card means that the child gets to take two more cards. Shuffle the "Take 2 Turns" cards into the stack. Help the child when he draws a "Take 2 Turns" card by having him draw one card, move his token, draw a second card, and

157

move his token again. Continue taking turns drawing cards and moving tokens until one player reaches the end.

Then start a new game. Show a "Move 3" and a "Move 4" card to the child. Explain that these cards mean you get to move forward three or four spaces. Shuffle the "Move 3" and "Move 4" cards into the stack. Help the child correctly follow each card's direction as you play the game. Continue taking turns drawing cards and moving tokens until one player reaches the end.

Dialogue Highlights

Talk about what you are doing. Here are some examples.

Level 1

- *Let's play a new game.*
- *Here are some new cards. This is a "Stop" card. It's red. Red means stop.*
- *This is a "Go" card. It's green. Green means go.*
- *When I pick the red card, I stop. I lose my turn.*
- *When I pick the green card, I go one space.*
- *Pick a card. You picked "Stop." What do you do?*

Level 2

- *This card says "Go Back." If you pick this card, you have to go back one space.*
- *Choose a card. You got a "Go" card. Move one space.*
- *I'll choose a card. My card says "Go Back." I'll move back one space.*
- *Your turn again.*

Level 3

- *With this card, we get to take two turns!*
- *I'll put it in the pile.*
- *It's your turn to pick a card.*
- *Wow! You got a "Take 2 Turns" card. You get to pick two more cards. Pick the first card. Move your token. That's right. Pick the second card. Move your token again.*
(Second game)
- *When you pick the "Move 3" card, you get to move ahead three spaces.*
- *When you pick the "Move 4" card, you get to move ahead four spaces.*

Extension Activity

To play a longer game, use the Game 3 card set with a commercial game board like CandyLand®. Return discarded game cards to the stack as needed. Continue until the first person reaches the end.

Promoting Peer Interaction   Board games are interactive by nature. Invite a friend/classmate of the child's to play. Guide them through the rules of a different board game than in *Games People Play 1* and *Games People Play 2*.

It's a Puzzle to Me

Skills
- putting puzzles together
- solving problems
- following directions
- improving hand-eye coordination

Materials
- 1 – 2 piece shape puzzle with non-interlocking pieces

Level 2
- 3 – 4 piece picture puzzle with non-interlocking pieces

Level 3
- 4 – 6 piece picture puzzle with interlocking pieces

Success Tips

Here are some specific strategies for putting puzzles together:
- Start by looking at the assembled puzzle. Talk about the features of the picture.
- Turn all puzzle pieces right-side up before beginning to assemble the puzzle.
- Direct the child to look for pieces with matching colors.
- Assemble specific objects or characters within the puzzle.
- Draw the child's attention to the shape of the puzzle piece edges.
- Encourage the child to choose a different puzzle piece if he has been unsuccessful with a puzzle piece for a long time.

Procedures

Level 1   Remove the pieces from a 1–2 piece shape puzzle. Show the child how to put the puzzle pieces in the correct places. Give the child a simple puzzle and let her practice putting in the pieces. Remind her to try another place or to turn the piece if the piece doesn't fit. You might help the child by guiding her hand.

Level 2   Give the child a 3–4 piece picture puzzle with non-interlocking pieces. Identify the picture on each puzzle piece. Then show the child how to fit the puzzle pieces into the holes as described above.

Level 3   Show the child a 4–6 piece puzzle with interlocking pieces. Show the child how the puzzle pieces fit together. Talk about the colors and shapes of the pieces that fit together. Then give the child the puzzle. Encourage him to take apart the puzzle and put it back together. Show the child how to try each piece in different places before putting it aside. Encourage him to keep trying until he finds the piece that fits.

Learning to put puzzles together requires patience. Plan enough time for the child to experiment and learn from mistakes.

Dialogue Highlights

Talk about what you are doing. Here are some examples.

Level 1

- *Here is a shape puzzle.*
- *I took out the circle and the square.*
- *I'll put the circle in. Now I'll put the square in.*
- *Let's do the puzzle again.*
- *Oh, the circle doesn't fit here.*
- *I'm turning the square to make it fit.*

Level 2

- *Here's a puzzle with four pieces.*
- *There's an apple. There's a banana. I see an orange and a pear too.*
- *I'll take the puzzle pieces out.*
- *The apple doesn't fit here.*
- *I'll put it in a different place.*
- *Now it's your turn. Put the pieces back into the puzzle.*

Level 3

- *This puzzle is a dog. There's his house.*
- *Take out the pieces.*
- *Start with the dog. The dog is black. Try it on the black side of the puzzle.*
- *It doesn't fit? Did you turn it?*
- *Try that piece later. Which piece will you try next?*

Extension Activity

Materials: crayons, paper, scissors

Have the child color pictures to make his own puzzles. Cut the pictures into pieces. Encourage the child to take apart and put together his puzzles. As a surprise, make a puzzle from a photograph of the child, his pet, or a family member.

Promoting Peer Interaction

Materials: puzzles

Divide a puzzle's pieces between two children. Ask the children to start by putting together specific objects or characters pictured in the puzzle. Prompt each child to ask the other child for pieces needed to complete the object or character. Have the children take turns until the puzzle is complete.

How Well Do You Stack Up?

Skills
- stacking blocks
- following directions
- using the preposition *on*
- counting
- playing games

Materials
- red, blue, and yellow blocks
- color coding labels (round stickers)

Levels 2 & 3
- a die with dots

Success Tips

You may want to use larger blocks for children just learning how to stack.

Build towers of two blocks side by side if the child has difficulty building a single block tower.

Procedures

Make a color "die." Take one block. Put one color-coding label on each side of the block using 2 red stickers, 2 blue stickers, and 2 yellow stickers. Show the child how to stack blocks.

Level 1	Start a stacking game by rolling the color "die." Point to and name the color that lands faceup. Choose a block that's the same color. Use this block to start the tower. Give the color die to the child. Help him roll the color die. Name the color that lands faceup. Help the child choose a block that's the same color. If the child can't find a block that matches, hold out two blocks for the child to choose between. Continue to roll the die and stack blocks until the tower falls. Keep track of how many blocks are in the tower. Challenge the child to make the tower taller each time you play.
Level 2	Modify the game by using numbers instead of colors to choose blocks for the tower. Have the child roll the die with dots. Help him count the number of dots that land faceup. Then help him choose the same number of blocks. Have him add the blocks one at a time to the tower. Ask the child to count with you as he adds blocks to the tower. Play until the tower falls.
Level 3	Have the child roll the color die and die with dots. Help him find blocks that match the color that lands faceup on the color die. Then help him count the number of blocks indicated on the die with dots. Have the child stack the blocks he counted. Stack blocks until the tower falls.

Dialogue Highlights

Talk about what you are doing. Here are some examples.

Level 1

- *I have some blocks.*
- *Watch me build a tower. I'm putting one block on top of the other.*
- *Now we'll do it together.*
- *First I roll the die.*
- *Red is on the top of the die.*
- *I'll find a red block.*
- *Your turn. Roll the die.*
- *Can you find a yellow block?*
- *Put your yellow block on top of the red block.*

Level 2

- *Let's play a stacking game.*
- *I'll roll the die. I'll count the dots. One, two, three. I need one, two, three blocks.*
- *I'll stack them.*
- *Now it's your turn.*
- *Roll the die. You rolled a four. One, two, three, four. Stack four blocks on top.*

Level 3

- *Let's stack these blocks.*
- *Roll both dice. You rolled the color yellow and the number four. Good, you counted four yellow blocks.*
- *Stack them up.*
- *It's my turn. Oops, our tower fell.*

Extension Activity

Materials: boxes, empty soda cans, and/or plastic containers, die

For more practice stacking, have the child stack boxes, empty soda pop cans, or plastic containers. Use the die with dots to determine the number of containers to stack. Encourage the child to make a castle or a city as he stacks the boxes, cans, and containers.

Promoting Peer Interaction

Materials: different-colored blocks, color die, die with dots

Give blocks of different colors to each child (one child gets red blocks, one gets yellow blocks). Have one child roll the color die and the die with dots. Ask the child to name the color that lands faceup on the color die and to identify who has that color of blocks. Next have the child count the dots faceup on the die and ask the player with the blocks for the correct number of blocks he needs. Encourage the child to stack the blocks before passing the dice to the next player. Play until the tower falls.

163

A Jar Full of Spoons

Skills

- improving hand-eye coordination
- using the prepositions *in* and *into*
- improving perception
- staying on task
- winning and losing graciously
- encouraging another person

Materials

- 3 clear jars: one with a small opening, one with a medium-sized opening, and one with a large opening
- 10 plastic spoons

Success Tip

At first, allow the child to hold the spoon below waist level to insure success. As the child masters the skill, have him hold the spoon at shoulder level before dropping into the jar.

Procedures

Level 1   Put the jar with the largest opening on the floor. Show the child how to aim and drop the spoons into the jar. Talk about what you're doing with the spoons. Then give the child five spoons for his turn at the jar. Ask the child to drop the spoons into the jar, one at a time. Cheer for the child. Continue practicing until the child can drop at least one spoon into the jar without help.

Level 2   Put the jar with the medium-sized opening on the floor. Show the child how to drop a spoon into the jar. Then give the child ten spoons to drop into the jar. If the child doesn't get any spoons into the jar, switch to a jar with a larger opening. Cheer for the child. Encourage the child to cheer for you when it's your turn. Anyone who drops two spoons into either jar is a "winner."

Level 3   Put the jar with the smallest opening on the floor. Give the child ten spoons to drop into the jar. As the child's skill increases, make the task more difficult. You might ask the child to stand on one leg or to cover one eye before dropping a spoon. Have the jars with larger openings available if needed. Cheer for the child. Encourage the child to cheer for you.

Dialogue Highlights

Talk about what you are doing. Here are some examples.

Level 1

- *I have a jar. I have some spoons.*
- *Watch. I'm going to drop a spoon into the jar.*
- *Oops! It didn't go into the jar.*
- *I'll try again.*
- *I did it.*
- *Your turn.*
- *You dropped the spoon.*
- *Good try!*

Level 2

- *Look! This jar is smaller.*
- *I'll try to drop a spoon into the jar.*
- *I missed! The spoon fell behind the jar.*
- *I'll try again. I did it! The spoon is in the jar!*
- *Let's see if you can drop a spoon in now.*
- *You dropped the spoon. Where did your spoon go?*

Level 3

- *Look. This jar is even smaller.*
- *Can you drop your spoon into the jar?*
- *Oops! Where did the spoon go this time?*
- *It went into the jar. Good job!*

Extension Activity

Materials: small objects of different weights and sizes like cotton balls, pennies, toothpicks, and pencils; jars with different-sized openings

Gather objects of different weights and sizes to drop into the jars. For a greater challenge, have the child use tongs to pick up and drop the objects into the jar.

Promoting Peer Interaction

Materials: spoons, jars with different-sized openings, blindfold

Explain the game to the children. Have the children practice dropping spoons into the jars. Blindfold one child. Ask the second child to guide the first child's arm and hand over a jar and tell him when to let go of the spoon. Then have the children switch roles.

To make this activity more challenging, tell the second child he cannot touch the first child. Ask the second child to tell the first child where to stand, where to put his arm and hand, and when to let go of the spoon.

On the Road Again

Skills
- following directions
- improving visual discrimination
- playing games
- improving attribute knowledge
- improving category knowledge
- counting

Materials
- none

Success Tip
While learning this game, it may be best to have each child look for a different object or place.

Procedures

Note: This game is played in a car.

Level 1   While driving a familiar route, tell the child to look for a specific object or place. Select an object or place you know will be along the route like a gas station, flag, swimming pool, or a friend's home. Have the child say "Bingo" when he sees the object or place. Practice until the child understands the task. Then have the child look for more than one object. Use common objects like traffic lights, stop signs, or buses.

Level 2   Have the child look for examples of a category like different animals, vehicles, or buildings. Count the number of objects the child sees in a category. During your next trip, look for objects in the same category. See how many objects the child finds during this trip. Compare the scores.

Level 3   Have the child look for an object or place with a specific characteristic like a big dog, a green truck, or a two-story house. Practice at this level until the child understands the task. Then explain that whenever you or the child sees the named object or place, you need to say "Bingo." Whoever says "Bingo" gets one point. Continue the game until one person earns five points.

Dialogue Highlights

Talk about what you are doing. Here are some examples.

Level 1
- *Let's play a game.*
- *I'll drive. You look out the window.*
- *Look for the gas station.*
- *Bingo! You found the gas station.*

(Second game)
- *Let's play a new game.*
- *Look for a stop sign. Say "Bingo" when you see a stop sign. There's a stop sign. Bingo!*
- *Look for another stop sign.*

Level 2
- *Yesterday we saw six dogs. Let's look for more today.*
- *Bingo! I see a dog by the tree. That's one.*
- *Keep looking.*
- *You saw a dog by the garage. That's two dogs.*

Level 3
- *Today let's look for trucks. We only count green trucks.*
- *Start looking.*

(Second game)
- *You're good at finding green trucks.*
- *Now if you see a green truck first, say "Bingo." Then you'll get a point. If I see a green truck first, I'll say "Bingo" and I'll get a point. We'll play until someone gets five points.*
- *Ready? Start looking.*

Extension Activity

Materials: catalogs or magazines

Name an item you have seen in the catalog or magazine. Tell the child to look for the item and to say "Bingo" when he finds it. Then tell the child to look for another example of the item or to look for a different item. Have the child cut out the picture of the item to keep "score."

Promoting Peer Interaction

Note: This activity can be done in a car, at home, or in a classroom.

Materials: books/magazines (optional)

Divide the children into pairs. Explain that you are going to have a contest. Name a specific object or place. Tell the children that each team member must see an example of the object or place. They can either look out the car window or look in books/magazines. One team member may help another team member find the object or place. The first team with both members finding an example of the object or place wins.

Game Board for Games People Play 1, 2, and 3

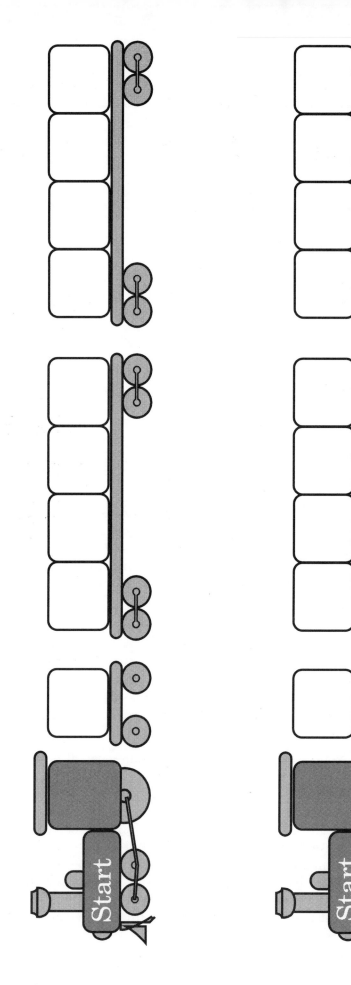

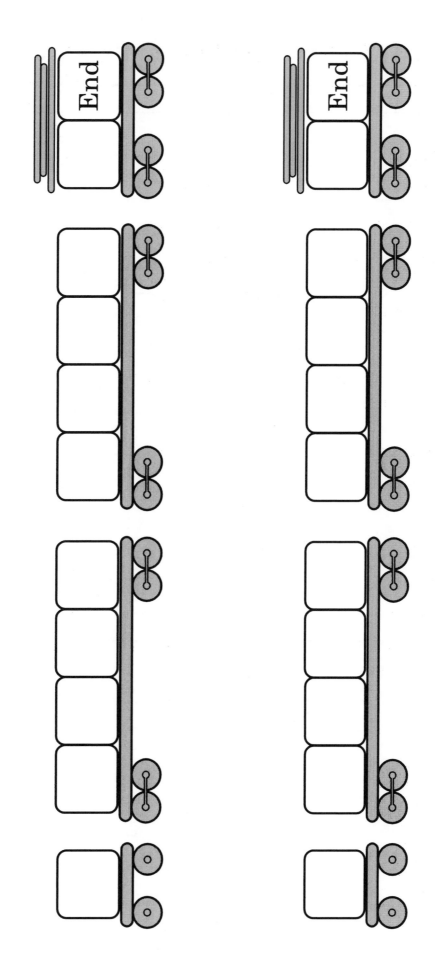

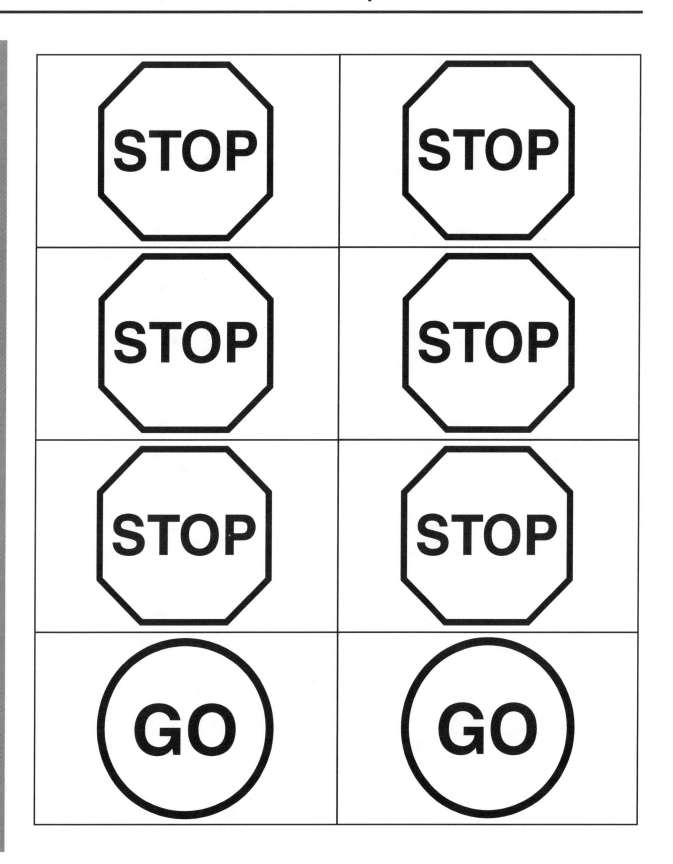

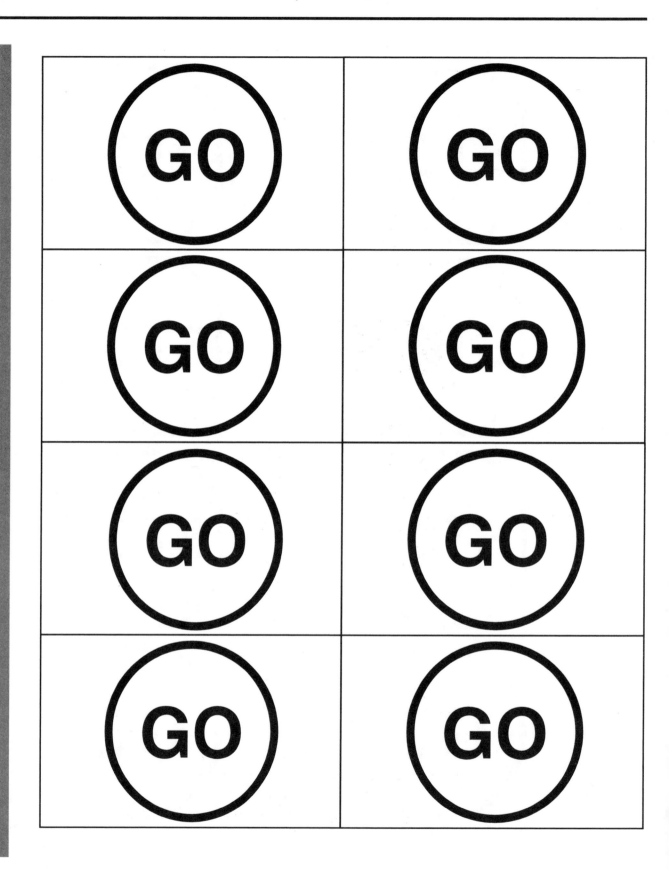

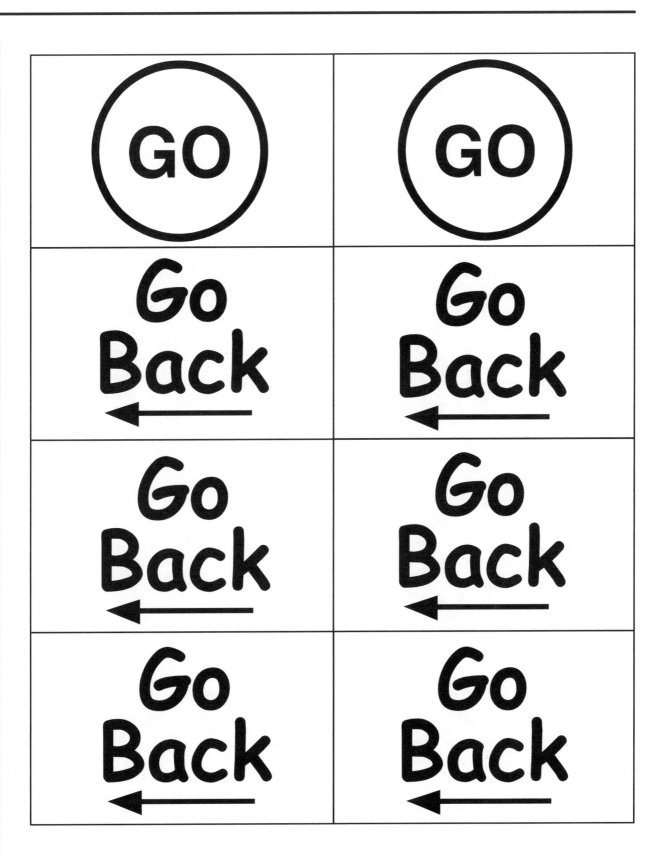

173

Take **2** Turns	Take **2** Turns
Take **2** Turns	Take **2** Turns
Take **2** Turns	Take **2** Turns
Move 3	Move 3

Move 3	Move 4
Move 4	Move 4

175

Suggested Books

To help you get started reading to children, we have included a list of our favorite children's books. While this list is by no means complete or exhaustive, it is intended to be a starting point. You may look for other books by the same author or other books of a similar style as you develop your own collection of favorites.

Beginning books are often small with cardboard pages. In many cardboard books, the pictures are of a baby with a common object or doing a common action. Others use fictional characters or have drawings rather than photographs as illustrations. Try to select books with one main object pictured per page.

Who Says Quack? published by Grossett & Dunlap
Red, Blue, Yellow Shoe by Tana Hoban
What Is It? by Tana Hoban
I Can Help by Margaret Miller
I See by Helen Oxenbury
Baby's ABC published by Random House
What Do Babies Do? published by Random House
What Do Toddlers Do? published by Random House
My Clothes by Sian Tucker

Some picture books focus on one subject throughout the book. *The Eye Openers Series* by Simon and Schuster and *My First Look At* by Random House may be effective for a child with a particular interest, like trucks or dogs. Picture books by Donald Crews like *Freight Train* or *School Bus* feature one subject in more detail.

First stories have repetitive text and illustrations that take up most of the page. They are about things familiar to children, like animals, toys, or daily activities.

Where's the Cat? by Stella Blackstone and Debbie Harter
Have You Seen My Cat? by Eric Carle
The Very Busy Spider by Eric Carle
Is Your Mama a Llama? by Deborah Guarino
The Doorbell Rang by Pat Hutchins
A-Hunting We Will Go by Stephen Kellogg
Brown Bear, Brown Bear, What Do You See? by Bill Martin Jr
I Went Walking by Sue Williams
Let's Go Visiting by Sue Williams

Some books build a story by adding lines, so that all previous lines of text are repeated on each page, like *The House that Jack Built* (traditional folk tale).

Shoes from Grandpa by Mem Fox
I Know an Old Lady illustrated by G. Brian Karras
Froggy Gets Dressed by Jonathan London
The Bag I'm Taking to Grandma's by Shirley Neitzel
The Dress I'll Wear to the Party by Shirley Neitzel

 　　　　　　　　　　　For Parents & Professionals: Preschool

The Jacket I Wear in the Snow by Shirley Neitzel
Big Pumpkin by Erica Silverman
The Napping House by Audrey Wood

When looking for "real stories" to read, start with books with a simple plot that describe a familiar life sequence.

Will I Have a Friend? by Miriam Cohen
When I Was Little by Jamie Lee Curtis
Jillian Jiggs by Phoebe Gilman
Tucking Mommy In by Morag Loh
If You Give a Mouse a Cookie by Laura Joffe Numeroff
Thomas' Snowsuit by Robert Munsch
Today I'm Going Fishing with My Dad by N.L. Sharp
When Mama Comes Home Tonight by Eileen Spinelli

Some books are especially good for reading aloud and lend themselves to be acted out by children.

Berlioz Bear by Jan Brett
Goldilocks and the Three Bears retold by Jan Brett
Three Billy Goats Gruff (traditional folk tale)
King Bidgood's in the Bathtub by Audrey Wood

Suggested Recordings of Children's Songs/Music

Using recordings of children's songs is an effective way to sing with your child. The recording helps keeps the beat and tune, and serves as a reminder for the words. As the child becomes comfortable with the song and learns the words, turn down the volume so the child can carry the song. You can also play the recording to get the child started and then turn it off, allowing the child to continue.

Check your local bookstore for these recordings. You can also contact Kaplan Company, Inc. at 1-800-334-2014 or *www.kaplanco.com* or Lakeshore Learning Materials at 1-800-421-5354 or *www.lakeshorelearning.com.*

Elle Jenkins
Early Early Childhood Songs
You'll Sing a Song and I'll Sing a Song

Hap Palmer
Getting to Know Myself
Learning Basic Skills Through Music: Building Vocabulary

Sharon, Lois, and Bram
Mainly Mother Goose
All the Fun You Can Sing

Steve and Greg
On the Move with Steve and Greg
Playin' Favorites

Wee Sing
Children's Songs and Fingerplays
Nursery Rhymes and Lullabies

Index of Activities and Skills

Index of Activities and Skills, *continued*

References

Anderson, R.C. et al. *Becoming a Nation of Readers: The Report of the Commission on Reading*. Washington, D.C.: National Academy of Education, 1985.

Brigance, A. H. *Brigance Diagnostic Inventory of Early Development*. North Billerica, MA: Curriculum Associates, 1978.

Chaille, C. and Silvern, S. B. "Understanding Through Play." *Childhood Education*, Vol. 72, No. 5, 1996.

Early Childhood Continuum of Assessment Programming Evaluation and Resources (CAPER). Sioux City, IA: Western Hills Area Education Agency, 1982.

Feldman, J.R. *Complete Handbook of Indoor and Outdoor Games and Activities for Young Children*. West Nyack, NY: The Center for Applied Research in Education, 1994.

Ford, S. A. "The Facilitator's Role in Children's Play." *Young Children*, Vol. 48, No. 6, 1993.

Gestwicki, C. *Developmentally Appropriate Practice: Curriculum and Development in Early Childhood Education*. Albany, NY: Delmar Publishers, Inc., 1995.

Hildebrand, V. *Guiding Young Children*. New York: MacMillan Publishing Co., Inc., 1980.

Jalongo, M.R. "Using Recorded Music with Young Children: A Guide for Non-Musicians." *Young Children*, Vol. 51, No. 5, 1996.

Kostelnik, M. J. et al. *Developmentally Appropriate Programs in Early Childhood Education*. New York: Macmillan Publishing Co., Inc., 1993.

Maffie, A. C. and Hauck, T. M. *Purposeful Play With Your Preschooler*. New York: Plenum Press, 1992.

Mitchell, A. and David, J. (eds.) *Explorations with Children, A Curriculum Guide from the Bank Street College of Education*. Beltsville, MD: Gryphon House, 1992.

Morrison, G. S. *Fundamentals of Early Childhood Education*. Upper Saddle River, NJ: Prentice-Hall, Inc., 1997.

Raines, S. *Never, EVER, Serve Sugary Snacks On Rainy Days: The Official Little Instruction Book for Teachers of Young Children*. Beltsville, MD: Gryphon House, Inc., 1995.

Seefeldt, C. (ed.). *The Early Childhood Curriculum, A Review of Current Research*. New York: Teachers College Press, 1992.

Van Scoy, I. J. and Fairchild, S. H. "It's About Time! Helping Preschool and Primary Children Understand Time Concepts." *Young Children,* Vol. 48, No. 2, 1993.

Ward, C. D. "Adult Intervention: Appropriate Strategies for Enriching the Quality of Children's Play." *Young Children*, Vol. 51, No. 3, 1996.

1-01-9876543

181